Kaplan Publishing … finding new ways to support students looking for exam … urces really do add an extra dimension …

This book com… resources so that you can study anytime, anyw… **… resource is not sold separately and is included in the … the book.**

Having purchased this book, you have access to the following online study materials:

CONTENT	AAT	
	Text	Kit
Electronic version of the book	✓	✓
Knowledge Check tests with instant answers	✓	
Mock assessments online	✓	✓
Material updates	✓	✓

How to access your online resources

Received this book as part of your Kaplan course?
If you have a MyKaplan account, your full online resources will be added automatically, in line with the information in your course confirmation email. If you've not used MyKaplan before, you'll be sent an activation email once your resources are ready.

Bought your book from Kaplan?
We'll automatically add your online resources to your MyKaplan account. If you've not used MyKaplan before, you'll be sent an activation email.

Bought your book from elsewhere?
Go to **www.mykaplan.co.uk/add-online-resources**
Enter the ISBN number found on the title page and back cover of this book.
Add the unique pass key number contained in the scratch panel below.
You may be required to enter additional information during this process to set up or confirm your account details.

This code can only be used once for the registration of this book online. This registration and your online content will expire when the examinations covered by this book have taken place. Please allow one hour from the time you submit your book details for us to process your request.

Please scratch the film to access your unique code.

Please be aware that this code is case-sensitive and you will need to include the dashes within the passcode, but not when entering the ISBN.

KAPLAN PUBLISHING

AAT

Q2022

Credit and Debt Management

EXAM KIT

This Study Text supports study for the following AAT qualifications:

AAT Level 4 Diploma in Professional Accounting
AAT Diploma in Professional Accounting at SCQF Level 8

KAPLAN
PUBLISHING

British Library Cataloguing-in-Publication Data

A catalogue record for this book is available from the British Library.

Published by:

Kaplan Publishing UK

Unit 2 The Business Centre

Molly Millar's Lane

Wokingham

Berkshire

RG41 2QZ

ISBN: 978-1-83996-595-1

Printed and bound in Great Britain

CONTENTS

Features in this revision kit

In addition to providing a wide ranging bank of real exam style questions, we have also included in this kit:

- Paper specific information and advice on exam technique.
- Our recommended approach to make your revision for this particular subject as effective as possible.

You will find a wealth of other resources to help you with your studies on the AAT website:

www.aat.org.uk/

Quality and accuracy are of the utmost importance to us so if you spot an error in any of our products, please send an email to mykaplanreporting@kaplan.com with full details.

Our Quality Co-ordinator will work with our technical team to verify the error and take action to ensure it is corrected in future editions.

UNIT SPECIFIC INFORMATION

THE EXAM

FORMAT OF THE ASSESSMENT

The assessment is divided into several standalone tasks which cover all of the learning outcomes and assessment criteria.

In any one assessment, students may not be assessed on all content, or on the full depth or breadth of a piece of content. The content assessed may change over time to ensure validity of assessment, but all assessment criteria will be tested over time.

The learning outcomes for this unit are as follows:

	Learning outcome	Weighting
1	Understand relevant legislation and contract law that impacts the credit control environment	15%
2	Understand how information is used to assess credit risk and grant credit in compliance with organisational policies and procedures	45%
3	Understand the organisation's credit control processes for managing and collecting debts	25%
4	Understand different techniques available to collect debts	15%
	Total	100%

Time allowed

2 hours

PASS MARK

The pass mark is 70

Always keep your eye on the clock and make sure you attempt all questions!

DETAILED SYLLABUS

The detailed syllabus and study guide written by the AAT can be found at:

www.aat.org.uk/

INDEX TO QUESTIONS AND ANSWERS

EXAM TECHNIQUE

- **Do not skip any of the material** in the syllabus.
- **Read each question very** carefully.
- **Double-check your answer** before committing yourself to it.
- Answer **every** question – if you do not know an answer to a multiple choice question or true/false question, you don't lose anything by guessing. Think carefully before you **guess**.
- If you are answering a multiple-choice question, **eliminate first those answers that you know are wrong**. Then choose the most appropriate answer from those that are left.
- **Don't panic** if you realise you've answered a question incorrectly. Getting one question wrong will not mean the difference between passing and failing.

Computer-based exams – tips

- Do not attempt a CBA until you have **completed all study material** relating to it.
- On the AAT website there is a CBA demonstration. It is **ESSENTIAL** that you attempt this before your real CBA. You will become familiar with how to move around the CBA screens and the way that questions are formatted, increasing your confidence and speed in the actual exam.
- Be sure you understand how to use the **software** before you start the exam. If in doubt, ask the assessment centre staff to explain it to you.
- Questions are **displayed on the screen** and answers are entered using keyboard and mouse. At the end of the exam, you are given a certificate showing the result you have achieved.
- In addition to the traditional multiple-choice question type, CBAs will also contain **other types of questions**, such as number entry questions, drag and drop, true/false, pick lists or drop down menus or hybrids of these.
- In some CBAs you will have to type in complete computations or written answers.
- You need to be sure you **know how to answer questions** of this type before you sit the exam, through practice.

KAPLAN'S RECOMMENDED REVISION APPROACH

QUESTION PRACTICE IS THE KEY TO SUCCESS

Success in professional examinations relies upon you acquiring a firm grasp of the required knowledge at the tuition phase. In order to be able to do the questions, knowledge is essential.

However, the difference between success and failure often hinges on your exam technique on the day and making the most of the revision phase of your studies.

The **Kaplan textbook** is the starting point, designed to provide the underpinning knowledge to tackle all questions. However, in the revision phase, poring over text books is not the answer.

Kaplan pocket notes are designed to help you quickly revise a topic area; however, you then need to practice questions. There is a need to progress to exam style questions as soon as possible and to tie your exam technique and technical knowledge together.

The importance of question practice cannot be over-emphasised.

The recommended approach below is designed by expert tutors in the field, in conjunction with their knowledge of the examiner and the specimen assessment.

You need to practise as many questions as possible in the time you have left.

OUR AIM

Our aim is to get you to the stage where you can attempt exam questions confidently, to time, in a closed book environment, with no supplementary help (i.e. to simulate the real examination experience).

Practising your exam technique is also vitally important for you to assess your progress and identify areas of weakness that may need more attention in the final run up to the examination.

In order to achieve this we recognise that initially you may feel the need to practice some questions with open book help.

Good exam technique is vital.

THE KAPLAN REVISION PLAN

Stage 1: Assess areas of strengths and weaknesses

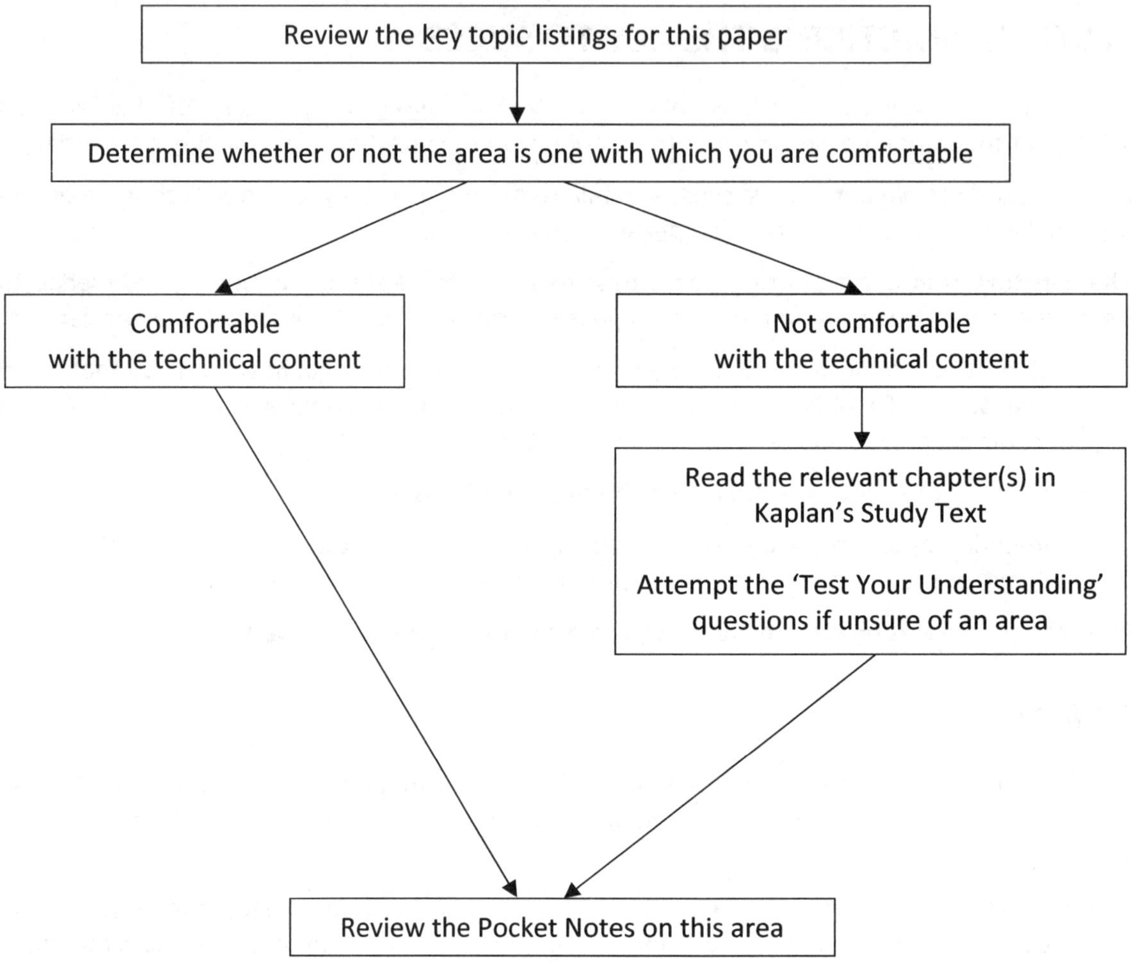

Stage 2: Practice questions

Follow the order of revision of topics as presented in this kit and attempt the questions in the order suggested.

Try to avoid referring to text books and notes and the model answer until you have completed your attempt.

Review your attempt with the model answer and assess how much of the answer you achieved.

Comfortable with question attempt

Only revisit when comfortable with questions on all topic areas

Not comfortable with question attempts

Focus on these areas by:

- Reworking 'Test your understanding' questions in Kaplan's Study Text
- Revisiting the technical content from Kaplan's Pocket Notes
- Working any remaining questions on that area in the Exam Kit

Stage 3: Final pre-exam revision

We recommend that you **attempt at least one two hour 30 minute mock examination** containing a set of previously unseen exam standard questions.

Attempt the mock CBA online in timed, closed book conditions to simulate the real exam experience.

Section 1

PRACTICE QUESTIONS

LEGISLATION

CONTRACT LAW FEATURES

1 **Identify whether the following statements about a contract are true or false.**

	True	False
A contract made by a company must be in writing.		
A contract of employment must be in writing.		

2 S wrote to B offering to sell certain garden plants for £50,000. B sent a written reply asking if payment could be made by instalments.

What is the legal effect of B's reply?

A B has made a counter offer

B B has accepted A's offer

C B has requested further information

D B has rejected the offer

3 **Identify whether the following statements relating to consideration are true or false?**

	True	False
A promise to perform an existing statutory duty is sufficient to amount to good consideration.		
A peppercorn is sufficient to amount to good consideration.		
Past consideration is sufficient to amount to good consideration.		

4 Alpha Limited receives a letter from Beta Limited containing an order for 100 kilograms of rice. Alpha sends Beta a schedule of standard conditions, which includes the clause that payment is due within 30 days of invoice date.

This clause is an example of:

A An invitation to treat

B Consideration

C An offer

D A misrepresentation

5 Which of the following is/are correct?

	True	**False**
A person who signs a contract is deemed to have read it.		
A person who signs a contract is bound by all its terms.		
A person who has not read a contract cannot be bound by it.		

6 The essential features of a valid simple contract are:

A Offer, acceptance and consideration only

B Offer, acceptance, consideration, intention to create legal relations and certainty of terms only

C Offer and acceptance only

D Offer, acceptance, intention to create legal relations only

7 Consideration need not be adequate but must be:

A Money

B Sufficient

C Of equivalent value to the goods

D Accepted

8 A contract entered into as a result of a misrepresentation is:

A Enforceable

B Voidable

C Void

D Absolutely valid

9 Which of the following is not an essential element of a valid simple contract?

A The contract must be in writing

B The parties must be in agreement

C Each party must provide consideration

D Each party must intend legal relations

10 Consideration is

A The intention of the parties to be legally bound

B The need for fairness in the contract

C The promise to exchange value

D The payment of cash

11 Davina is the owner of a boutique. She places a notice in the window advertising the sale of dresses at half price.

The notice is:

A A contractual offer

B A completed contract

C An acceptance of an offer

D An invitation to treat

12 Retention of title is:

A The right of the purchaser to retain ownership of the goods received.

B The right of the seller to retain ownership of the goods until a cheque has been posted.

C The right of the seller to retain ownership of the goods until payment is made.

D The right of the purchaser to expect that title is retained by the seller even when payment has been received.

13 Which of the following are features of a simple contract (tick all that apply)?

	Tick
Offer.	
Consideration.	
Acceptance.	
Intention to create legal relations.	
Invitation to treat.	

14 Simon is ordering a pizza on the telephone and says he will pay when he picks up the order. Which of the following would constitute consideration?

A Placing the order

B Paying for the order

C Saying he will pay for the order

D Picking up the order

15 A void contract is a contract that:

A Cannot be enforced by the law

B Can be enforced by the law

C Can be nullified

D Is valid

16 Which of the following is not a feature of a simple contract?

A Offer

B Consideration

C Intention to create legal relations

D Invitation to treat

17 Which of the following is NOT an essential element of a valid simple contract?

A The contract must be in writing

B The parties must be in agreement

C Each party must provide consideration

D Each party must intend legal relations

18 A voidable contract is a contract that:

A Cannot be enforced by the law

B Is frustrated

C Can be nullified

D Is valid

19 Which of the following statements are not true?

A Consideration needs to be adequate but not sufficient

B Consideration can be executory, executed but not past

C Executory consideration is the promise to do something in the future in exchange for another promise to be done in the future

D Executed consideration is when the promise is actually executed, in exchange for another promise to be executed in the future

CONTRACT LAW APPLICATION

20 Jose orders a pizza by telephone and says he will pay on delivery. Which of the following would constitute consideration?

A Calling the pizza restaurant

B Handing over money to the pizza delivery person

C Accepting delivery of the pizza

D Promising to pay for the pizza

21 S Ltd displays a video telephone in its shop window priced at £199. Yasmin goes into the shop and says she will buy the video telephone for £199. S Ltd says it has been wrongly priced and refuses to sell it.

Which of the following is correct?

A A contract has been made between S Ltd and Yasmin

B No contract has been made because Yasmin makes an offer to S Ltd which S Ltd has rejected

C No contract has been made because Yasmin makes a counter-offer which S Ltd has rejected

D No contract has been made because there is no offer

22 Office Supplies Ltd placed the following advertisement in a local newspaper:

'Special offer! We are able to offer for sale a number of 3.1m pixel top-of-the-range digital cameras at a specially reduced price of £25.90. Order now while stocks last.'

The advertisement contained a mistake in that the cameras should have been priced at £259.00. B plc immediately placed an order for 50 cameras.

Which of the following is correct?

A Office Supplies Ltd can refuse to supply B plc as the advertisement is not an offer, but an invitation to treat

B As B plc has not yet paid for the cameras, it has no contractual right to them

C Office Supplies Ltd can only refuse to sell the cameras to B plc if it has sold its entire inventory

D B plc has accepted an offer and is contractually entitled to the 50 cameras

23 On Saturday X and Y made a contract for the sale of X's car to Y. It was agreed that Y would have immediate delivery but that Y need not pay the price until the end of the month.

Which of the following is correct?

A The consideration given by Y is executory consideration

B If Y fails to pay the price at the end of the month, the contract is voidable

C The consideration given by Y is insufficient to amount to good consideration because it is past

D If Y fails to pay the price at the end of the month, the contract is void

24 Decor Ltd contracted to fit out a shop for Suremarket plc, with the shop to be ready for use by a set date. Due to Decor Ltd's lack of adherence to safety requirements, the Health and Safety Executive have issued a notice prohibiting further work on the site until safety measures as per its improvement notice are implemented by Decor Ltd.

Which of the following gives the correct position?

A Decor Ltd can increase the contract price to cover the costs of implementing the safety measures.

B Decor Ltd will be in breach of contract if it fails to complete the fitting out by the set date.

C If Decor Ltd fails to complete the fitting out by the set date it will not be in breach of contract provided it can show that it has taken all reasonable steps to do so.

D The contract between Decor Ltd and Suremarket plc is frustrated if the actions of the Health and Safety Executive mean that it is impossible to complete the fitting out by the set date.

25 **Which of the following is not a remedy for breach of contract?**

A Damages

B A decree of specific performance

C Action for the price

D A fine

26 'For sale – Computer, monitor and laser printer. Good condition. £500.'

What is the legal effect of the following statement in a newspaper?

A The statement is an offer for sale

B The statement is a 'mere puff or boast'

C The statement has no legal effect

D The statement is an invitation to treat

27 A Ltd placed the following advertisement in a local newspaper:

'We are able to offer for sale a number of portable colour television sets at the specially reduced price of £5.90. Order now while stocks last.'

The advertisement contained a mistake in that the television sets should have been priced at £59.00. B Ltd immediately placed an order for 100 television sets.

Which one of the following statements is correct?

A A Ltd has accepted an offer and is contractually entitled to the 100 television sets.

B A Ltd can refuse to supply B Ltd as the advertisement is not an offer, but an invitation to treat.

C A Ltd can only refuse to sell the television sets to B Ltd if it has sold all its inventory.

D As B Ltd has not yet paid for the television sets, the company has no contractual right to them.

28 Kai sends a letter to Emily on 1 January offering to buy Emily's antique Ming vase for £1,000. On the same day Emily sends a letter to Kai offering to sell to Kai the same antique Ming vase for £1,000.

Kai now changes his mind and wishes to know the likely legal position.

A There is a valid contract; Kai and Emily have reached agreement and waived the need for acceptance.

B Both have made offers on the same terms and no acceptance is necessary.

C There is agreement but no contract, since neither Kai nor Emily knew that their offers had been accepted.

D There is a contract but is lacks consideration since neither Kai nor Emily has paid a price for the other's promise.

29 Adrian places an advert in a newspaper 'car for sale £1,000'. Brenda telephones him and asks if Adrian will accept £900.

(i) Adrian's advert is an offer.

(ii) Brenda's telephone call is a counter offer.

Which of the above is/are correct?

A Both (i) and (ii)

B Neither (i) nor (ii)

C (ii) only

D (i) only

30 **Which of the following statements made in the negotiations preceding a contract will be classed as a misrepresentation if it subsequently proves to be false?**

A No woman can resist a man who wears this perfume

B We should launch the product in North America next autumn

C In our opinion your investment will grow and grow

D The television will receive digital channels without further modification

31 Anaya shops at a supermarket.

A contract is formed when:

A Anaya pays for her shopping

B Anaya puts her selection in the trolley

C The checkout assistant takes Anaya's goods

D Anaya picks up items from the shelves

32 Doug receives a letter from Paul containing an order of 50 kg of sugar for £100.

Which of the following statements is correct?

A Paul's letter is an invitation to treat and Doug's response that he can supply the sugar is an offer.

B Paul's letter is an offer and Doug's response that he can supply the sugar is an acceptance.

C Paul's letter is an acceptance and Doug's response that he cannot supply the sugar is a breach of contract.

D Paul's letter is an acceptance and Doug's response that he can supply the sugar is consideration.

33 Ekta asks Bob for a price to paint her kitchen. Bob says he can do it for £500 and Ekta says that will be fine. Halfway through the work Bob asks for an additional sum of £200 because he underestimated the work.

Which of the following statements are correct?

A Ekta must pay Bob the £200 because the agreement was made in good faith and Bob made a mistake.

B Bob cannot force Ekta to pay the additional amount because the agreement was for £500.

C Bob can force Ekta to pay because she never accepted the price.

D If Ekta refuses to pay Bob can simply work until he has done £500 worth of painting.

34 **Alex has a notice in her shop window saying that the cameras he has for sale are now discounted by 40%. This is an example of:**

A Consideration

B Offer

C Acceptance

D Invitation to treat

35 PC Universe Ltd placed the following advertisement in a computer magazine.

'Sale! We are able to offer for sale a number of 4GB top-of-the-range computers at a specially reduced price of £150. Order now while stocks last.'

The advertisement contained a mistake in that the computers should have been priced at £1500. The local school immediately placed an order for 30 computers.

Which of the following is correct?

A PC Universe Ltd can only refuse to sell the cameras to the school if it has sold its entire inventory.

B As the school has not yet paid for the computers, it has no contractual right to them.

C The school has accepted an offer and is contractually entitled to the 30 computers.

D PC Universe Ltd can refuse to supply the school as the advertisement is not an offer, but an invitation to treat.

36 Alice wrote to Hamza offering to sell him her car for £5,000. Hamza sent an email reply asking if payment could be made by cheque.

What is the legal effect of Hamza's reply?

A Hamza has made a counter offer

B Hamza has accepted Alice's offer

C Hamza has rejected the offer

D Hamza has requested further information

37 RTC is an information technology support company. There is a signed contract with PP to provide IT support for 6 months which started on the 1st July. The normal daily charge is £550 but RTC have agreed to charge £500 per day subject to a minimum of 60 days support. PP determines the number of days worked each month.

A total of 45 days of support have been provided during July to November. The total invoiced so far is £22,500. A further 10 days of support have been provided in December.

How much should RTC invoice PP in December?

A £5,000

B £5,500

C £7,500

D £8,250

CONTRACT LAW REMEDIES

38 A customer owes £4,800 including VAT and the debt is 50 days late. The current Bank of England base rate is 1.5%. Calculate the interest charge under the Late Payments of Commercial Debts Act rounding down to the nearest penny.

£

39 Mary orders some clothing which are advertised as being 100% pure new wool. When she received the goods the label says 60% wool and 40% Polyester.

Mary has a claim for breach of contract due to:

A Fiduciary misconduct

B Misrepresentation

C Misuse of Sales Act

D Unfair Contract Terms Act

40 Buyer bought a pair of underpants from Retailer Ltd. Unknown to both Buyer and Retailer Ltd there were unsafe chemical residues in the underpants and when Buyer wore them they suffered a nasty rash. Buyer now wishes to sue Retailer Ltd for damages for breach of contract.

Which of the following is correct?

A Buyer will succeed because the underpants were not of satisfactory quality.

B Buyer will not succeed because Retailer Ltd did not know that the underpants were not of satisfactory quality.

C Buyer will succeed only if they can prove that Retailer Ltd was negligent.

D Buyer will succeed only if they can prove that it was Retailer Ltd's fault that the underpants were not of satisfactory quality.

41 A gardening firm is contracted to cut grass and tidy the cuttings away in a public park. The gardening firm consistently leaves the grass cuttings on the paths. The public authority successfully sues the gardening firm for breach of contract and the judge instructs the gardening firm to finish the work.

This is an example of:

A An action for price

B An action for goods

C An action for specific performance

D An action for remedy

42 Buyer bought some flowerpots from Seller Ltd over the Internet. Due to a mistake by the website's designer, the flowerpots were described as 12 inches in diameter whereas in reality the flowerpots are only 12 cm in diameter. Buyer now wishes to return the flowerpots to Seller Ltd and get their money back on the ground of breach of contract.

Which of the following is correct?

A Buyer has a right to return the flowerpots to Seller Ltd and get their money back because the flowerpots did not correspond with the description.

B Buyer has a right to return the flowerpots to Seller Ltd and get their money back only if they can prove that Seller Ltd knew of the mis-description and had done nothing to correct it.

C Buyer has no action against Seller Ltd; their action is against the website designer.

D Buyer has no right to return the flowerpots to Seller Ltd and get their money back because the rule when buying over the Internet is 'let the buyer beware'.

43 IT Ltd was under contract to install an integrated computer system in all ten of Distributor plc's premises for a price of £1m. After completing the installation in nine of the premises, IT Ltd abandoned the project because its financial problems prevented it from purchasing further materials.

Which of the following is correct?

A IT Ltd is entitled to nothing.

B IT Ltd has substantially performed the contract and is entitled to a reasonable sum in respect of the work done.

C IT Ltd has completed 90% of the work and is, therefore, entitled to £900,000.

D The contract between IT Ltd and Distributor plc is frustrated.

44 Zed plc contracted to hire a hotel for its annual general meeting. If the hotel becomes unavailable on the date, which of the following would provide the hotel owner with a lawful excuse for non-performance of the contract?

	True	**False**
The hotel is double-booked.		
The hotel is struck by lightning and burns down.		
The authorities order the closure of the hotel because of non-compliance with safety regulations.		

45 In the event of a breach of contract what is the purpose of damages?

(i) To ensure that the contract breaker does not profit from their breach.

(ii) To punish the contract breaker.

(iii) To put the innocent party in the same position they would have been in had the contract been properly performed.

Options:

A (i) only

B (ii) only

C (iii) only

D (i) and (iii) only

46 Which of the following statements in relation to damages for breach of contract is/are correct?

(i) Damages are not normally awarded for personal injury.

(ii) Damages are not normally awarded for loss of profits.

(iii) Damages are not normally awarded for loss of enjoyment and distress.

Options:

A (i) only

B (ii) only

C (iii) only

D (ii) and (iii) only

47 John advertised his car for sale at £20,000. Petra saw the advertisement and wrote to John offering him £20,000. John did not reply and sold the car to Gabriel for £21,000. Petra wishes to sue John for breach of contract.

What is the legal position?

A John is liable. Petra had accepted John's offer to sell for £20,000.

B John is not liable. Petra had made an offer and this was not accepted by John.

C John is liable. He should have communicated to Petra the fact that Petra's offer had not been accepted.

D John is not liable. Petra must actually communicate her offer in person.

48 (i) A customer owes £2,000 excluding VAT and the debt is 30 days late. The current Bank of England base rate is 2.5%. Calculate the interest charge under the Late Payments of Commercial Debts Act to the nearest penny.

£

(ii) How much additional compensation can be claimed as a fixed sum to help cover the costs of collecting this overdue commercial debt?

A £20

B £40

C £70

D £100

49 Damages in contract are awarded with a view to:

A Putting the innocent parties in the position in which they would have been if the contract had been performed.

B Putting the innocent parties in the position in which they would have been if the contract had never been made.

C Putting the innocent parties in the position in which they would have been if the contract had been performed plus a sum to provide compensation.

D Putting the innocent parties in the position in which they would have been if the contract had never been made plus a sum to provide compensation.

50 Legal action can be taken against a customer for non-payment of an invoice when:

A There is a contract in existence and the non-payment is a breach of contract

B There is no contract in existence but the payment is still due

C There is a contract in existence and the non-payment is a misrepresentation

D There is a contract in existence and the non-payment is a remedy

51 The normal remedy for breach of contract due to non-payment of the debt is:

A An action for specific performance

B An action for price

C An action for remedy

D An action for the goods

52 Which of the following statements in relation to remedies for breach of contract are correct?

	Tick
The injured party may recover damages for any loss suffered.	
The injured party may force the other party to complete the contract.	
The injured party may bring an 'action for price'.	
The injured party may fine the other party.	

53 The late payment act allows businesses to charge other business customers interest on overdue amounts. The 'statutory interest' rate chargeable is:

A Bank of England base rate + 8%

B Bank of England base rate + 5%

C Bank of England base rate + 3%

D Bank of England base rate + 10%

54 Which of the following is the definition of a fundamental breach of contract?

A one party refuses to complete their side of the contract

B one party has breached a condition of the contract

C one party completely fails to complete the contract

D one party informs the other party prior to the due date that the contract will not be completed

DATA PROTECTION ACT

55 The Data Protection Act applies to:

A All records held by the company

B Only manual records

C Only computer records

D Only records of opinions

56 The Data Protection Act applies to:

A Data about individuals only

B Data about individuals, companies and government departments

C Data about companies only

D Data about individuals and companies only

57 Under the Data Protection Act processing of personal data is forbidden except in which of the following circumstances?

(i) With the consent of the individual.

(ii) Due to a legal obligation.

(iii) In the public interest.

(iv) To protect the vital interests of the individual.

Options:

A (i) only

B (ii) and (iv)

C (ii) and (iii) only

D All of them

58 Under the Data Protection Act the individuals whose information is being held can:

	Tick
Have access to a copy of the data held.	
Ask to know why the data is being processed.	
Seek compensation through the courts for damage or distress caused by the loss, destruction, inaccuracy or unauthorised disclosure of their data.	
Apply to the courts or Registrar for inaccurate data to be corrected or removed from their files.	

OTHER LEGISLATION

59 In a contract for the sale of goods by a business to a consumer, any attempt to exclude the term implied by the Consumer Rights Act that goods sold in the course of a business must be of satisfactory quality is:

A Void

B Void unless reasonable

C Voidable at the option of the consumer

D Valid if the consumer has signed the contract

60 Identify whether the following statements about a contract are true or false.

	True	False
The Consumer Rights Act allows a buyer to return faulty goods within 30 days and receive a full refund		
Under the Consumer Rights Act, a fault is presumed to have existed at purchase if the faulty goods are returned within three month of purchase		
The Consumer Credit Act gives additional protection on purchases of between £100 and £30,000 made with a debit or credit card		
The Trade Descriptions Act applies to both goods and services		

61 Steve bought a jar of chicken korma sauce from the local supermarket, but when he opens the jar it is actually sweet and sour sauce. Steve can claim for breach of contact due to:

A Unfair Contract Terms Act

B Misuse of Sales Act

C Misrepresentation

D Fiduciary misconduct

62 The Trade Descriptions Act states that:

A Contracts must be written in language that is understandable

B Manufacturers, retailers and the service industry must correctly describe what they are selling

C The seller has the right to be selling the goods/providing the service

D The goods are of 'satisfactory quality'

63 Which of the following are the statutory rights stated by the Consumer Rights Act

(i) That the goods are fit for purpose.

(ii) That the goods match the description provided by the seller.

(iii) The goods are of satisfactory quality.

Options:

A (i) only

B (ii) only

C (i) and (iii) only

D All of them

GRANTING CREDIT

GRANTING CREDIT PROCEDURES

64 Clare Ltd is a potential new customer and has approached Rhoda Ltd to ask for a credit limit of £25,000. The sales director has advised you that she has invited the directors of Clare Ltd to go to the races next month as is keen to gain Clare's business. The sales director is paid a bonus on any new business she attracts.

Write notes explaining three sources of external information you would use to assess the credit status of Clare Ltd (other than financial statements). Comment on the sales director's actions.

65 Side Ltd sells nuts, bolts, screws and related items to plumbers.

You work for the finance team at Side Ltd. Over the last few years Side Ltd has suffered because a couple of their customers have ceased trading, causing Side Ltd to have to write off their unpaid accounts.

The company has a team of sales representatives who call on customers. Their main role is to check that customers are satisfied with the service they receive and encourage them to buy more products. The Finance Manager is aware that sales representatives regularly call on customers. She has asked you how the sales representatives could add credit control tasks to their visits.

Side Ltd employs an Accounts Receivable Clerk. She records all credit sales and all payments by customers. She also prints an aged receivables analysis every Monday morning and gives it to the Finance Manager. There is no Credit Controller. The Finance Manager would like the accounts receivables clerk to carry out additional tasks that would reduce the risk of Side having to write off more debts.

(a) **Write notes to the Finance Manage to identify two tasks that sales representatives could carry out that would assist credit control. Explain how each task would assist credit control within Side Ltd.**

(b) **Write notes to brief the Accounts Receivable Clerk to identify three tasks that the clerk could carry out that would reduce the risk of Side Ltd having to write off more debts. Explain how each task wold help reduce the risk.**

66 **When taking up bank references the bank usually provides one of 3 types of references. Which of the following is not a standard bank reference?**

A Unqualified, positive

B Qualified, positive

C General indication

D Guarded

67 In gathering credit information on a potential client you would use both internal sources of credit information and external sources of credit information.

Which of the following are examples of internal or external information?

	Internal	External
Trade references.		
Sales representatives' knowledge.		
Credit Agency.		
Bank references.		
Supplier references.		
Ratio calculations.		

68 **Which of the following are possible reasons for refusing to grant credit to a potential customer?**

(i) Poor trade references.

(ii) Poor credit agency report.

(iii) Lack of historical financial statements due to customer recently starting to trade.

(iv) Not wanting to lose the company as a customer.

Options:

A (i) and (ii) only

B (i), (ii) and (iii) only

C (ii) and (iii) only

D All of the above

69 **Which of the following are possible reasons for refusing to grant credit to a potential customer?**

(i) Trade references not available.

(ii) An unqualified report from the bank.

(iii) A quick ratio of less than 1.

(iv) Trade payable days that are less than the credit terms.

Options:

A (i) and (ii) only

B (i) and (iv) only

C (i) and (iii) only

D (ii) and (iv) only

70 Refusal of credit terms should be communicated to the customer:

(i) by letter

(ii) with reasons for refusal

(iii) explaining that trading is not possible at present

(iv) courteously

Options:

A (i) only

B (i) and (iii) only

C (i), (ii) and (iii) only

D (i), (ii) and (iv) only

71 Which of the following is not a method of analysing credit control information?

A Aged payable analysis

B Trading history

C 80/20 rule

D Materiality

72 Which of the following is a method of analysing credit control information?

A Aged trade payables analysis

B Pareto's Principle

C Trade journals

D Gearing ratio

73 Which of the following information could be used to assess the credit status of a new customer?

	Tick
Financial accounts	
Aged receivable analysis	
Copies of outstanding invoices	
Draft contract for trade	
Trade references	
Bank references	

74 You are unable to grant credit to a customer at the moment due to the customer being a new business and having no history. Write a letter explaining why you are unable to grant credit but encouraging them to trade with you.

PERFORMANCE INDICATORS

75 Which of the following is a benefit of ratio analysis when using it to decide whether to offer credit to a customer?

A Only one year's statistics is required

B The accounts are a true representation of the company going forwards

C The final accounts of a business should be easily accessible

D Statistics are a very good source of information

76 When analysing a set of accounts which of the following ratios would be of most interest to the credit controller?

A Quick ratio

B Payable days

C Return on capital employed

D Gross profit margin

77 The quick ratio is an example of a measure of:

A Liquidity

B Profitability

C Debt

D Cash flow

78 Which of the following are suitable options for the blank in the following inventory days formula – Inventory/[blank] × 365?

(i) Cost of sales.

(ii) Cash sales.

(iii) Credit purchases.

(iv) Cash purchases.

Options:

A (i) only

B (ii) and (iv) only

C (i) and (iii) only

D (iii) and (iv) only

Use the following information for Questions 79 – 85.

Extracts from a company's accounts show the following balances:

	£000		£000
Inventories	150	Revenue	2,700
Receivables	300	Cost of sales	1,300
Cash	25	Gross profit	1,400
Payables	230	Admin costs	500
Overdraft	90	Distribution costs	350
		Operating profit	550
		Finance cost	75

79 Which of the following is the company's current ratio, calculated to the nearest two decimal places?

A 1.48

B 1.41

C 1.96

D 1.02

80 Which of the following is the company's quick ratio (acid test), calculated to the nearest two decimal places?

A 1.41

B 1.02

C 1.48

D 1.30

81 Which of the following is the receivables' payment period in days (to the nearest day)?

A 41 days

B 84 days

C 78 days

D 45 days

82 Which of the following is the payables' payment period in days (to the nearest day)?

A 31 days

B 65 days

C 60 days

D 35 days

83 What is the inventory holding period (to the nearest day)?

A 4 days

B 10 days

C 24 days

D 42 days

84 What is the operating profit margin of the company?

A 52%

B 39%

C 20%

D 25%

85 What is the interest cover of the company?

A 4.67 times

B 5.67 times

C 7.33 times

Use the following information for Questions 86 – 90.

Extracts from a company's accounts show the following:

	£000	£000
Non-Current assets		33,000
Current assets		
Inventory	22,000	
Trade receivables	12,506	
Cash	5,006	
		39,512
Total assets		**72,512**
Equity		
Share capital		100
Revaluation reserve		12,000
Retained earnings		26,412
Non-current liabilities		
Loans		16,000
Current liabilities		
Trade payables		15,000
Overdraft		3,000
Total equity and liabilities		**72,512**

Additional Notes	£000
Revenue	64,323
Profit before interest and taxation	27,657
Profit before tax	23,598

86 What is the gearing ratio of the company?

A 29.4%

B 33.0%

C 41.5%

D 57.1%

87 Which of the following is the company's operating margin?

[ ] %

88 Which of the following is the company's quick ratio (acid test), calculated to the nearest two decimal places?

A 0.83

B 1.27

C 0.97

D 2.57

89 Which of the following is the ROCE of the company (return on capital employed)?

A 72%

B 92%

C 47%

D 51%

90 What are the receivable days of the company (to the nearest whole day)?

A 14 days

B 18 days

C 71 days

D 90 days

Use the following information for Questions 91 – 98.

Extracts from a company's accounts show the following:

Statement of profit or loss	£000		Statement of financial position	£000	£000
Revenue	2,250		Non-current assets		700
Cost of sales	1,000		Current assets		
Gross profit	1,250		Inventory	150	
Distribution costs	275		Trade receivables	240	
Administrations	150		Cash	100	
Operating profit	825				490
Finance cost	80		Long term loans		200
Profit before Tax	745		Trade payables		275
Tax	90				
Profit for the year	655				

91 What is the gross profit margin?

A 55.6%

B 36.7%

C 33.1%

D 29.1%

92 What is the operating profit margin?

A 55.6%

B 36.7%

C 33.1%

D 29.1%

93 What is the current ratio?

A 1.2

B 0.9

C 1.4

D 1.8

94 What are the receivable days?

A 88 days

B 80 days

C 70 days

D 39 days

95 What are the payable days?

A 100 days

B 80 days

C 143 days

D 45 days

96 What is the inventory turnover in days?

A 24 days

B 55 days

C 44 days

D 66 days

97 The accounts of Pony, which has a year end of 30 June, show a receivables figure of £60,000. Revenue for the year amounted to £350,000, of which £50,000 were cash sales.

The trade receivables collection period during the year in question was:

A 63 days

B 73 days

C 83 days

D 97 days

98 Ben has been trading with Jerry for many years. Jerry purchased 5,500 units of a product prices at £8 per unit including VAT. At the 31 December 20X4 Jerry owed Ben £2,600.

The receivable collection period in days for the amount owing by Jerry is [ ] days

CREDIT LIMIT ASSESSMENT (RATING SYSTEM)

99 You work as a credit control manager for Gallop Limited which uses a credit rating system to assess the credit status of new and existing customers.

The credit rating (scoring) system table below is used to assess the risk of default by calculating key indicators (ratios), comparing them to the table and calculating an aggregate score.

Credit rating (scoring) system	**Score**	**Credit rating (scoring) system**	**Score**
Operating profit margin		**Current ratio**	
Losses	–5	less than 1	–20
Less than 5%	0	between 1 and 1.25	–10
5% and above but less than 10%	5	between 1.25 and 1.5	0
10% and above but less than 20%	10	above 1.5	10
More than 20%	20	**Gearing**	
Interest cover		less than 25%	20
No cover	–30	25% and above but less than 50%	10
Less than 1	–20	more than 50% less than 65%	0
More than 1 but less than 2	–10	between 65% and 75%	–20
More than 2 but less than 4	0	between 75% and 80%	–40
More than 4	10	above 80%	–100

Risk	**Aggregate score**
Very low risk	Between 60 and 21
Low risk	Between 20 and 1
Medium risk	Between 0 and –24
High risk	Between –25 and –50
Very high risk	Above –50

The sales department has asked for a credit limit of £30,000 to be given to Trot Limited who is a potential new customer. Financial information has been supplied by Trot Limited.

Accounts for Trot Limited **Statement of profit or loss**	**20X2**	**20X1**	**Statement of financial position**	**20X2**	**20X1**
	£000	£000		£000	£000
Revenue	**9,000**	**11,000**	**Non-current assets**		
Cost of sales	7,000	7,600	Property, plant and equipment	**4,400**	**5,000**
Gross profit	**2,000**	**3,400**	**Current Assets**		
Distribution costs	2,100	2,300	Inventory	1,800	1,500
Administration costs	2,000	2,000	Trade Receivables	2,000	1,700
Operating profit	**–2,100**	**–900**	Cash	100	800
Finance cost	200	100		**3,900**	**4,000**
Profit before taxation	**–2,300**	**–1,000**	**Total assets**	**8,300**	**9,000**
Tax	0	0	**Equity**		
Profit for the year	**–2,300**	**–1,000**	Share capital	400	400
			Retained earnings	1,700	4,000
			Non-current liabilities		
			Loans	2,000	1,000
			Current liabilities		
			Trade payables	4,200	3,600
			Total equity and liabilities	**8,300**	**9,000**

(a) Complete the table below by calculating the key indicators (to two decimal places) for 20X2 and 20X1 for Trot Limited, and rate the company using the credit rating scoring system.

Trot Limited	**Indicator**	**Rating**	**Indicator**	**Rating**
Year	**20X2**		**20X1**	
Operating profit margin				
Interest cover				
Current ratio				
Gearing				
Total				

(b) Based on the result of your credit rating and the table below, comment whether the requested credit limit should be given to Trot Limited.

Rating	Decision
Very low or low risk current year and very low or low risk previous year	Accept
Very low or low risk current year and medium risk previous year	Accept
Very low or low risk current year and high or very high risk previous year	Request latest management accounts and defer decision
Very high risk or high risk current year	Reject
Medium risk current year and medium, low or very low risk previous year	Accept
Medium risk current year and high or very high risk previous year	Accept

A Accept

B Request latest management accounts and defer decision

C Reject

100 You work as a credit control manager for Gallop Limited which uses a credit rating system to assess the credit status of new and existing customers.

The credit rating (scoring) system table below is used to assess the risk of default by calculating key indicators (ratios), comparing them to the table and calculating an aggregate score.

Credit rating (scoring) system	Score	Credit rating (scoring) system	Score
Operating profit margin		**Current ratio**	
Losses	–5	less than 1	–20
Less than 5%	0	between 1 and 1.25	–10
5% and above but less than 10%	5	between 1.25 and 1.5	0
10% and above but less than 20%	10	above 1.5	10
More than 20%	20	**Gearing**	
Interest cover		less than 25%	20
No cover	–30	25% and above but less than 50%	10
Less than 1	–20	more than 50% less than 65%	0
More than 1 but less than 2	–10	between 65% and 75%	–20
More than 2 but less than 4	0	between 75% and 80%	–40
More than 4	10	above 80%	–100

Risk	**Aggregate score**
Very low risk	Between 60 and 21
Low risk	Between 20 and 1
Medium risk	Between 0 and –24
High risk	Between –25 and –50
Very high risk	Above –50

The sales department has asked for a credit limit of £50,000 to be given to Walk Limited who is a potential new customer. The financial information below has been supplied by Walk Limited.

Accounts for Walk Limited Statement of profit or loss	**20X2**	**20X1**	**Statement of financial position**	**20X2**	**20X1**
	£000	£000		£000	£000
Revenue	**22,500**	**20,000**	**Non-current assets**		
Cost of sales	15,625	15,000	Property, plant and equipment	**11,250**	**9,750**
Gross profit	**6,875**	**5,000**	**Current assets**		
Distribution costs	2,125	2,125	Inventory	3,000	2,500
Administration costs	1,500	1,500	Trade receivables	1,750	1,500
Operating profit	**3,250**	**1,375**	Cash	1,000	1,000
Finance cost	625	625		**5,750**	**5,000**
Profit before taxation	**2,625**	**750**	**Total assets**	**17,000**	**14,750**
Tax	875	250	**Equity**		
Profit for the year	**1,750**	**500**	Share capital	250	250
			Retained earnings	6,750	5,000
			Non-current liabilities		
			Loans	6,250	6,250
			Current liabilities		
			Trade payables	3,750	3,250
			Total equity and liabilities	**17,000**	**14,750**

(a) **Complete the table below by calculating the key indicators (to two decimal places) for 20X2 and 20X1 for Walk Limited, and rate the company using the credit rating scoring system.**

Walk Limited	**Indicator**	**Rating**	**Indicator**	**Rating**
Year	**20X2**		**20X1**	
Operating profit margin				
Interest cover				
Current ratio				
Gearing				
Total				

(b) Based on the result of your credit rating and the table below, comment whether the requested credit limit should be given to Trot Limited.

Rating	Decision
Very low or low risk current year and very low or low risk previous year	Accept
Very low or low risk current year and medium risk previous year	Accept
Very low or low risk current year and high or very high risk previous year	Request latest management accounts and defer decision
Very high risk or high risk current year	Reject
Medium risk current year and medium, low or very low risk previous year	Accept
Medium risk current year and high or very high risk previous year	Accept

A Accept

B Request latest management accounts and defer decision

C Reject

101 You work as a credit control manager for Gallop Limited which uses a credit rating system to assess the credit status of new and existing customers.

The credit rating (scoring) system table below is used to assess the risk of default by calculating key indicators (ratios), comparing them to the table and calculating an aggregate score.

Credit rating (scoring) system	Score	Credit rating (scoring) system	Score
Operating profit margin		**Current ratio**	
Losses	–5	less than 1	–20
Less than 5%	0	between 1 and 1.25	–10
5% and above but less than 10%	5	between 1.25 and 1.5	0
10% and above but less than 20%	10	above 1.5	10
More than 20%	20	**Gearing**	
Interest cover		less than 25%	20
No cover	–30	25% and above but less than 50%	10
Less than 1	–20	more than 50% less than 65%	0
More than 1 but less than 2	–10	between 65% and 75%	–20
More than 2 but less than 4	0	between 75% and 80%	–40
More than 4	10	above 80%	–100

Risk	**Aggregate score**
Very low risk	Between 60 and 21
Low risk	Between 20 and 1
Medium risk	Between 0 and –24
High risk	Between –25 and –50
Very high risk	Above –50

Canter Limited has been trading with Gallop Limited for several years and has, until recently, always paid to terms. Following several late payments they have now contacted Gallop Limited to request an increase in their credit limit from £50,000 to £100,000. Canter Limited has supplied the accounts below.

Accounts for Canter Limited Statement of profit or loss	**20X1**	**20X0**	**Statement of financial position**	**20X1**	**20X0**
	£000	£000		£000	£000
Revenue	**9,750**	**9,000**	**Non-current assets**		
Cost of sales	6,900	5,700	Property, plant and equipment	**10,575**	**6,525**
Gross profit	**2,850**	**3,300**	**Current assets**		
Distribution costs	1,275	1,275	Inventory	1,800	825
Administration costs	900	900	Trade receivables	1,950	1,200
Operating profit	**675**	**1,125**	Cash	150	450
Finance cost	750	375		**3,900**	**2,475**
Profit before taxation	**–75**	**750**	**Total assets**	**14,475**	**9,000**
Tax	0	225	**Equity**		
Profit for the year	**–75**	**525**	Share capital	150	150
			Retained earnings	3,675	3,750
			Non-current liabilities		
			Long term loans	7,500	3,000
			Payables		
			Trade payables	3,150	2,100
			Total equity and liabilities	**14,475**	**9,000**

Additional information supplied by the sales department after a visit to Canter Limited.

Canter Limited has recently acquired several new large customers and therefore purchased new assets with long term loans to ensure that forecast sales demands can be met. The contracts with new the customers were only completed in the second half of the year and it is expected that sales will continue to increase in 20X2 with little increase in costs because the new machines have resulted in a reduction in variable cost per unit. The directors of Canter Limited expect a profit after tax in 20X2 of around £500,000. In anticipation of orders for 20X2 Canter Limited significantly increased its inventory levels at the end of 20X1.

(a) Complete the table below by calculating the key indicators (to two decimal places) for 20X1 and 20X0 for Canter Limited, and rate the company using the credit rating scoring system.

Canter Limited	Indicator	Rating	Indicator	Rating
Year	20X1		20X0	
Operating profit margin				
Interest cover				
Current ratio				
Gearing				
Total				

(b) Based on the result of your credit rating and taking into account the trading history and additional information supplied by the sales department, recommend a course of action.

You could make use of additional terms in the contract or any other options open to Canter Limited which could provide additional comfort.

102 You work as a credit control manager for Cardinal Limited which uses a credit rating system to assess the credit status of new and existing customers.

The credit rating (scoring) system table below is used to assess the risk of default by calculating key indicators (ratios), comparing them to the table and calculating an aggregate score.

Credit rating (scoring) system	Score	Credit rating (scoring) system	Score
Operating profit margin		**Quick ratio**	
Losses	–10	Less than 0.5	–20
Less than 5%	0	More than or equal to 0.5 but less than 1	–10
5% and above but less than 10%	10	More than or equal to 1 but less than 1.5	0
10% or above	20	1.5 or above	10
Interest cover		**Gearing**	
No cover	–30	less than 30%	10
Less than 1	–20	more than or equal to 30% but less than 40%	0
More than or equal to 1 but less than 2	–10	more than or equal to 40% but less than 50%	–20
More than or equal to 2 but less than 3	0	50% or above	–40
3 or above	10		

Risk	**Aggregate score**
Very low risk	Higher than 20
Low risk	Between 20 and 1
Medium risk	Between 0 and –24
High risk	Between –25 and –50
Very high risk	Worse than –50

The sales department has asked for a credit limit of £100,000 to be given to B Limited who is a potential new customer. The financial information below has been supplied by B Limited.

B Limited Statement of profit or loss	**20X1**	**20X0**	**Statement of financial position**	**20X1**	**20X0**
	£000	£000		£000	£000
Revenue	**9,000**	**7,000**	**Non-current assets**		
Cost of sales	4,000	3,000	Property, plant and equipment	**5,000**	**4,500**
Gross profit	**5,000**	**4,000**	**Current assets**		
Distribution costs	1,350	1,150	Inventory	600	500
Administration costs	2,200	1,500	Trade Receivables	1,200	900
Operating profit	**1,450**	**1,350**	Cash	480	400
Finance cost	250	250		**2,280**	**1,800**
Profit before taxation	**1,200**	**1,100**	**Total assets**	**7,280**	**6,300**
Tax	320	300	**Equity**		
Profit for the year	**880**	**800**	Share capital	100	100
			Retained earnings	3,580	2,700
				3,680	**2,800**
			Non-current liabilities		
			Long term loans	3,000	3,000
			Current liabilities		
			Trade payables	600	500
			Total equity and liabilities	**7,280**	**6,300**

(a) Complete the table below by calculating the key indicators (to two decimal places) for 20X1 and 20X0 for B Limited, and rate the company using the credit rating scoring system.

B Limited	**Indicator**	**Rating**	**Indicator**	**Rating**
Year	**20X1**		**20X0**	
Operating profit margin				
Interest cover				
Quick ratio				
Gearing				
Total				

(b) Based on the result of your credit rating and the table below, comment whether the requested credit limit should be given to Trot Limited.

Rating	Decision
Very low or low risk current year and very low or low risk previous year	Accept
Very low or low risk current year and medium risk previous year	Accept
Very low or low risk current year and high or very high risk previous year	Request latest management accounts and defer decision
Very high risk or high risk current year	Reject
Medium risk current year and medium, low or very low risk previous year	Accept
Medium risk current year and high or very high risk previous year	Accept

A Accept

B Request latest management accounts and defer decision

C Reject

103 You work as a credit control manager for Thomville Limited which uses a credit rating system to assess the credit status of new and existing customers.

The credit rating (scoring) system table below is used to assess the risk of default by calculating key indicators (ratios), comparing them to the table and calculating an aggregate score.

Credit rating (scoring) system	Score	Credit rating (scoring) system	Score
Operating profit margin		**Acid test ratio**	
Losses	–30	Less than 0.5	–60
Less than 5%	0	More than or equal to 0.5 but less than 1	–30
5% and above but less than 10%	30	More than or equal to 1 but less than 1.5	0
10% or above	60	1.5 or above	30
Interest cover		**Gearing**	
No cover	–90	less than 30%	30
Less than 1	–60	more than or equal to30% but less than 35%	0
More than or equal to 1 but less than 2	–30	more than or equal to 35% but less than 45%	–60
More than or equal to 2 but less than 3	0	45% or above	–120
3 or above	60		

Risk	**Aggregate score**
Very low risk	Higher than 60
Low risk	Between 60 and 1
Medium risk	Between 0 and –74
High risk	Between –75 and –150
Very high risk	Worse than –150

The sales department has asked for the credit limit of Oville Limited, an existing customer, to be extended from £40,000 to £80,000. The financial information below has been supplied by Oville Limited.

Accounts for Oville Limited Statement of profit or loss	**20X1** £000	**20X0** £000	**Statement of financial position**	**20X1** £000	**20X0** £000
Revenue	**8,000**	**5,200**	**Non-current assets**		
Cost of sales	6,200	4,000	Property, plant and equipment	**3,850**	**2,625**
Gross profit	**1,800**	**1,200**	**Current assets**		
Distribution costs	800	600	Inventory	1,400	630
Administration costs	600	450	Trade receivables	1,750	1,225
Operating profit	**400**	**150**	Cash	0	175
Finance cost	150	50		**3,150**	**2,030**
Profit before taxation	**250**	**100**	**Total assets**	**7,000**	**4,655**
Tax	30	28	**Equity**		
Profit for the year	**220**	**72**	Share capital	400	400
			Retained earnings	2,100	1,880
				2,500	**2,280**
			Non-current liabilities		
			Loans	1,750	875
			Current liabilities		
			Trade payables	2,100	1,400
			Overdraft	650	100
				2,750	**1,500**
			Total equity and liabilities	**7,000**	**4,655**

(a) **Complete the table below by calculating the key indicators (to two decimal places) for 20X1 and 20X0 for Oville Limited, and rate the company using the credit rating scoring system.**

Oville Limited	**Indicator**	**Rating**	**Indicator**	**Rating**
Year	**20X1**		**20X0**	
Operating profit margin %				
Interest cover				
Acid test				
Gearing %				
Total				

(b) Based on the result of your credit rating and the table below, comment whether the requested credit limit should be given to Trot Limited.

Rating	Decision
Very low or low risk current year and very low or low risk previous year	Accept
Very low or low risk current year and medium risk previous year	Accept
Very low or low risk current year and high or very high risk previous year	Request latest management accounts and defer decision
Very high risk or high risk current year	Reject
Medium risk current year and medium, low or very low risk previous year	Accept
Medium risk current year and high or very high risk previous year	Accept

A Accept

B Request latest management accounts and defer decision

C Reject

104 You work as a credit control manager for Frazier Limited which uses a credit rating system to assess the credit status of new and existing customers.

The credit rating (scoring) system table below is used to assess the risk of default by calculating key indicators (ratios), comparing them to the table and calculating an aggregate score.

Credit rating (scoring) system	Score	Credit rating (scoring) system	Score
Operating profit margin		**EBITDA/Total debt**	
Losses	–5	0.6 and above	20
Less than 5%	0	0.3 and above but less than 0.6	10
5% and above but less than 10%	5	0.125 and above but less than 0.3	0
10% and above but less than 20%	10	0.1 and above but less than 0.125	–10
20% and over	20	0.05 and above but less than 0.1	–20
Payable days		less than 0.05	–50
90 days or above	–20	**Interest cover**	
More than 60 but less than 90 days	–10	No cover	–30
More than 30 days but less than 60 days	0	Less than 1	–20
Less than 30 days	10	1 and above but less than 2	–10
		2 and above but less than 4	0
		More than 4	10

Risk	**Aggregate score**
Very low risk	Higher than 20
Low risk	Between 20 and 1
Medium risk	Between 0 and –24
High risk	Between –25 and –50
Very high risk	Worse than –50

Note:

Only companies with low or very low risk are normally granted credit. Companies with medium risk may be granted credit subject to further considerations.

The sales department has asked for the credit limit of Foreman Limited, an existing customer, to be extended from £50,000 to £250,000. The financial information below has been supplied by Foreman Limited.

Accounts for Foreman Limited	**20X1**	**20X0**
	£000	£000
Revenue	**12,000**	**10,000**
Cost of sales	5,500	4,000
Gross profit	**6,500**	**6,000**
Distribution costs	2,000	2,000
Administration costs	2,500	2,000
Operating profit	**2,000**	**2,000**
Finance cost	1,500	1,000
Profit before taxation	**500**	**1,000**
Tax	200	300
Profit for the year	**300**	**700**

Notes relating to Foreman's accounts

1 Depreciation included in Administration costs totalled £800,000 in 20X1 and £500,000 in 20X0.

2 Trade payables at the year end were £1,000,000 (20X1) and £700,000 (20X0).

3 Year end total debt was £5,000,000 (20X1) and £3,000,000 (20X0).

(a) Complete the table below to rate Foreman

Foreman Limited	**Indicator**	**Rating**	**Indicator**	**Rating**
Year	**20X1**		**20X0**	
Operating profit margin				
Trade payables days				
EBITDA/Total debt				
Interest cover				
Total score				

The sales department has asked for a credit limit of £100,000 to be given to Clay Limited who is a potential new customer. The financial information below has been supplied by Clay Limited.

Accounts for Clay Limited	**20X1**	**20X0**
	£000	£000
Revenue	**7,000**	**6,000**
Cost of sales	2,500	2,000
Gross profit	**4,500**	**4,000**
Distribution costs	1,100	1,000
Administration costs	700	750
Operating profit	**2,700**	**2,250**
Finance cost	1,700	1,500
Profit before taxation	**1,000**	**750**
Tax	50	50
Profit for the year	**950**	**700**

Notes relating to Clay's year end accounts

1 Depreciation included in Administration costs totalled £300,000 in 20X1 and £350,000 in 20X0.

2 Trade payables at the year end were £700,000 (20X1) and £600,000 (20X0).

3 Year end total debt was £4,500,000 (for both 20X1 and 20X0).

(b) Complete the table below to rate Clay.

Clay Limited	**Indicator**	**Rating**	**Indicator**	**Rating**
Year	**20X1**		**20X0**	
Operating profit margin				
Trade payables days				
EBITDA/Total debt				
Interest cover				
Total score				

(c) Based on the result of your credit rating, comment whether the requested credit limit should be given to Foreman or Clay Limited.

105 Explain the following ratios, including how you would use them to decide if a company can be granted credit:

1 Current ratio

2 Receivables' collection period in days

3 Payables' payment period in days

4 Inventory holding period in days

5 Operating Profit Margin

6 Interest Cover

7 Gearing

106 You work as a credit control manager for Wrong Limited and you have been asked to provide a credit limit of £10,000 for Wright Limited.

Wright Limited have provided you with a copy of their accounts.

Statement of profit or loss	**20X1** £	**20X0** £	**Statement of financial position**	**20X1** £	**20X0** £
Revenue	350,000	230,000	Non-current assets	150,000	30,000
Cost of sales	227,500	149,500	Current assets		
Gross profit	122,500	80,500	Inventory	25,690	18,164
Distribution costs	25,000	20,000	Trade receivables	62,789	41,918
Administration costs	50,000	45,000	Cash	35,878	500
Operating profit	47,500	15,500		124,357	60,582
Finance cost	5,000	5,000	**Total assets**	**274,357**	**90,582**
Tax	6,000	5,000	Equity		
Profit after tax	36,500	5,500	Share capital	160,100	100
			Retained earnings	53,318	22,318
			Non-current liabilities		
			Long term loans	15,000	50,000
			Current liabilities		
			Short term loan	21,959	–
			Trade payables	23,980	18,164
			Total equity and liabilities	**274,357**	**90,582**

Calculate the following ratios for both years and comment on whether you would give this company credit:

1 Operating profit margin

2 Interest cover

3 Current ratio

4 Receivables collection period in days

5 Payables' payment period in days

6 Gearing ratio

107 The draft accounts for Red Kite Ltd for the years ended 30th September 20X0 and 20X1 are as follows:

Statement of financial position	**20X1** £	**20X0** £
Non-current assets		
Premises	250,000	150,000
Plant	260,000	140,000
	510,000	**290,000**
Current assets		
Inventory	240,000	200,000
Receivables	160,000	120,000
	400,000	**320,000**
Total assets	**910,000**	**610,000**
Equity		
£1 ordinary shares	200,000	100,000
Share premium	180,000	70,000
Retained earnings	270,000	240,000
	650,000	**410,000**
Non-current liabilities		
7% Debentures	100,000	100,000
Current liabilities		
Trade payables	90,000	60,000
Bank overdraft	30,000	10,000
Taxation	40,000	30,000
	160,000	**100,000**
Total equity and liabilities	**910,000**	**610,000**

Statement of profit or loss	**20X1** £	**20X0** £
Revenue	**1,050,000**	**850,000**
Cost of sales	628,000	513,000
Gross profit	**422,000**	**337,000**
Distribution and administration expenses	315,000	255,000
Operating profit	**107,000**	**82,000**
Finance cost	7,000	7,000
Profit before taxation	**100,000**	**75,000**
Taxation	40,000	30,000
Profit after taxation	**60,000**	**45,000**
Dividends	30,000	20,000
Profit for the year	**30,000**	**25,000**

For the above company, calculate the following ratios for 20X0 and 20X1, and comment on the performance of the company:

1 Gross profit % (gross margin)

2 Operating profit % (operating margin)

3 Return on capital employed

4 Current ratio

5 Quick or acid test ratio

6 Receivable days

7 Payable days

108 You work as a credit control manager for Cardinal Limited which uses a credit rating system to assess the credit status of new and existing customers.

A Limited has been trading with Cardinal Limited for several years and has, until recently, always paid to terms. Following several late payments they have now contacted Cardinal Limited to request an increase in their credit limit from £40,000 to £80,000. The financial information below has been supplied by A Limited.

Accounts for A Limited	**20X1** £000	**20X0** £000
Revenue	**4,000**	**2,600**
Cost of sales	3,100	2,000
Gross profit	**900**	**600**
Distribution costs	400	300
Administration costs	250	200
Operating profit	**250**	**100**
Finance cost	100	50
Profit before taxation	**150**	**50**
Tax	40	14
Profit for the year	**110**	**36**

Statement of financial position	**20X1** £000	**20X0** £000
Non-current assets		
Property, plant and equipment	**2,200**	**1,500**
Current assets		
Inventory	800	360
Trade Receivables	1,000	700
Cash	0	100
	1,800	**1,160**
Total assets	**4,000**	**2,660**
Equity		
Share capital	200	200
Retained earnings	1,270	1,160
	1,470	**1,360**
Non-current liabilities		
Long term loans	1,000	500
Current liabilities		
Trade payables	1,200	800
Overdraft	330	0
	1,530	**800**
Total equity and liabilities	**4,000**	**2,660**

A Limited	**20X1**	**20X0**
Gross profit margin %	22.5	23.1
Operating profit margin %	6.3	3.8
Interest cover	2.5	2.0
Current ratio	1.18	1.45
Trade payable payment period in days	141	146
Trade receivables collection period in days	91	98
Inventory holding period in days	94	66
Gearing %	40.5	26.9

The sales manager has reviewed the latest information provided by A Limited and has made the following comments:

1 The company turnover has increased by 54% from £2.6 million to £4 million. This is a strong sign of overtrading.

2 The operating profit has increased from £100,000 to £250,000. This means that more cash is available to pay debts.

3 The interest cover has increased from 2.0 to 2.5 times which means that the company is in a worse position than last year.

4 The current ratio should be 2 which means that the company is insolvent.

5 The trade receivables balance has increased by £300,000 which supports the conclusion of overtrading.

6 The trade payables are down from 146 days to 141 implying the company is struggling to get credit from its suppliers.

7 The inventory has increased by £440,000 which supports the conclusion of overtrading.

8 Gearing has increased which means that the banks are not happy to lend money to the business.

9 My conclusion is that credit should not be given.

Required:

Write a brief note dealing with each comment that the sales manager has made. Explain any other indicators which aid the conclusion you make as to whether credit should be given.

109 Clare Ltd is a potential new customer and has approached Rhoda Ltd to ask for a credit limit of £25,000.

Rhoda Ltd has standard terms of trade of 30 days.

Clare Ltd has supplied the following information based on the last two years of trading.

Clare Limited Statement of profit or loss	**20X1**	**20X0**
	£000	£000
Sales Revenue	14,170	14,690
Cost of sales	11,180	11,605
Gross profit	**2,990**	**3,085**
Distribution costs	1,290	1,050
Administration costs	675	625
Operating profit	**1,025**	**1,410**
Finance cost	242	762
Profit before taxation	**783**	**648**
Tax	188	136
Profit for the year	**595**	**512**

Clare Limited Statement of financial position	**20X1**	**20X0**
ASSETS	£000	£000
Non-current assets		
Property, plant and equipment	**4,200**	**7,737**
Current assets		
Inventory	429	573
Trade Receivables	1,204	1,328
Cash	3	3
	1,636	**1,904**
Total assets	**5,836**	**9,641**
EQUITY AND LIABILITIES		
Equity		
Share capital	1,250	1,250
Retained earnings	1,162	568
Total equity	**2,412**	**1,818**
Non-current liabilities		
Borrowing	1,913	5,100
Current liabilities		
Trade and other payables	1,073	1,337
Taxation	188	136
Borrowing	250	1,250
	1,511	**2,723**
Total liabilities	**3,424**	**7,823**
Total equity and liabilities	**5,836**	**9,641**

Clare Limited	**20X1**	**20X0**
Gross profit margin%	21.1	21.0
Operating profit margin %	7.23	9.60
Interest cover	4.24	1.85
Current ratio	1.08	0.70
Trade payables payment period in days	35.0	42.1
Trade receivables collection period in days	31.0	33.0
Inventory holding period in days	14.01	18.02
Gearing %	44.23	73.72

The following additional information has also been provided.

Clare Ltd sells agricultural supplies, but also hires out larger machinery. Up to 20X0, the plant and equipment was purchased using finance leases. From 20X1 machinery was acquired using short term leases.

Commitments under short term leases are disclosed by way of a note to the financial statements:

Short term lease note	**20X1**	**20X0**
	£000	£000
Annual commitments under non-cancellable short term leases which expire:		
Within one year	1,055	100
In the second to fifth year inclusive	4,675	400
Over five years	215	0

Required:

Write a note analysing the information and recommending whether credit should be granted.

110 You work as a credit control manager for Thomville Limited which uses a credit rating system to assess the credit status of new and existing customers.

The sales department has asked for a credit limit of £100,000 to be given to Nicville Limited who is a potential new customer. The financial information below has been supplied by Nicville Limited.

Accounts for Nicville Limited Statement of profit or loss	**20X1**	**20X0**	**Statement of financial position**	**20X1**	**20X0**
	£000	£000		£000	£000
Revenue	**8,000**	**6,000**	**Non-current assets**		
Cost of sales	3,500	2,500	Property, plant and equipment	**4,000**	**3,500**
Gross profit	**4,500**	**3,500**	**Current assets**		
Distribution costs	1,000	800	Inventory	600	400
Administration costs	2,000	1,500	Trade receivables	1,300	950
Operating profit	**1,500**	**1,200**	Cash	250	300
Finance cost	400	250		**2,150**	**1,650**
Profit before taxation	**1,100**	**950**	**Total assets**	**6,150**	**5,150**
Tax	300	200	**Equity**		
Profit for the year	**800**	**750**	Share capital	100	100
			Retained earnings	2,250	1,350
				2,350	**1,450**
			Non-current liabilities		
			Long term loans	3,100	3,100
			Current liabilities		
			Trade payables	700	600
			Total equity and liabilities	**6,150**	**5,150**

The accounts have been analysed as follows:

Nicville Limited	**20X1**	**20X0**
Operating profit margin %	18.75	20.00
Interest cover	3.75	4.80
Quick ratio (Acid test)	2.21	2.08
Gearing %	56.88	68.13

Required:

Produce a report that details whether Nicville should be offered credit. Include more indicators if it will aid the decision.

111 The sales department has asked for a credit limit of £10,000 to be given to Grenouille Limited who is a potential new customer. The financial information below has been supplied by Grenouille Limited.

Statement of profit or loss	**20X1**	**20X0**	**Statement of financial position**	**20X1**	**20X0**
	£000	£000		£000	£000
Revenue	**10,000**	**6,000**	**Non-current assets**		
Cost of sales	6,000	4,000	Property, plant and equipment	5,800	5,750
Gross profit	**4,000**	**2,000**	**Current assets**		
Distribution costs	1,000	300	Inventory	1,300	450
Administration costs	1,200	400	Trade receivables	1,300	750
Operating profit	**1,800**	**1,300**	Cash	700	300
Finance costs	200	150	**Total assets**	**9,100**	**7,250**
Profit before taxation	**1,600**	**1,150**	**Equity**		
Tax	500	350	Share capital	600	600
Profit for the year	**1,100**	**800**	Retained earnings	3,300	2,200
			Total equity	**3,900**	**2,800**
			Non-current liabilities		
			Loans	4,400	4,000
			Current liabilities		
			Trade payables	800	450
			Total equity and liabilities	**9,100**	**7,250**

(a) **Complete the table below by calculating the key indicators (to 2 decimal places unless stated) for 20X0 and 20X1.**

Grenouille Limited	**20X1 Indicator**	**20X0 Indicator**
Gross profit margin %		
Operating profit margin %		
Trade payable days (to the nearest day)		
Inventory holding days (to the nearest day)		
Current ratio		

(b) Complete the email to the chief credit controller commenting on the ratios calculated in (a) above and conclude by recommending whether or not credit should be extended.

*** delete the wrong answers.**

Email

To: Credit controller **Date:** Today

From: AAT technician **Subject:** New customer Grenouille Limited

Please find below my observations and recommendations for new customer Grenouille limited.

Profitability

The revenue has increased by [   ]% which means that the company has either sold more units or increased the price of its product/increased sales which means the company is overtrading/cut its price to increase demand*.

The gross profit margin has increased by [   ] %.

The company may have increased the sales price of the product to increase demand/ increased the sales price of the product and or reduced the cost of production/decreased the sales price and increased the cost of the product*.

The most important indicator for profitability is the operating profit margin/gross profit margin/current ratio* which has reduced by 3.67%/16.94 %/20.39%*.

This is a good sign showing that the company is profitable/This is a bad sign because the company will become loss making/This is a warning sign because falling margins are always a concern/This is not a concern because the absolute profits have increased substantially*.

Liquidity

The current ratio provides a rough measure of the short term solvency of the organisation/a measure of long term liquidity/a measure of insolvency*.

In this case it has increased and is less than 4 which is a sign of insolvency/less than 2 which is a sign of insolvency/greater than 1 which is not a good sign as the current ratio should always be less than 1/greater than previous years which is a sign of improved solvency.

The inventory holding period has decreased/increased*. This appears to be fine/This appears to be a strong sign of overtrading/This is a concern because when revenue grows inventory levels should reduce*.

The trade payables payment period in days has increased/decreased* by [   ] days.

It appears that the company is funding its expansion in working capital by increasing trade payables/It appears that the company is funding its expansion in working capital by increasing inventory levels/It appears that the company is funding its expansion by increasing long term borrowings and retaining profit*.

I recommend that credit be granted/credit not be granted*.

112 Mungojerry Ltd has a standard application form that it requires customers to complete when they are applying for an increase to their credit limit. The following application form has been received from Rumpleteazer, who has been a customer for 9 months.

Application for an increase in credit limit			
Business name:	Rumpleteazer		
Current credit limit:	£17,000		
Requested new credit limit:	£40,000		
Accounts period	**31 August 20X3**	**31 August 20X2**	**Notes**
Sales revenue	£3,600,000	£2,000,000	Sales team have been on a motivation course.
Trade receivables	£690,300	£230,000	Credit controller has left the company.
Trade receivables collection period in days	70 days	42 days	Credit terms have been extended to 60 days.
Cost of sales	£2,730,000	£1,400,000	
Trade payables	£479,000	£134,000	
Trade payables payment period in days	64 days	35 days	
Inventories	£490,000	£138,000	Inventory increased due to increase in sales demand.
Inventories holding period in days	66 days	36 days	
Gross profit	£870,000	£600,000	
Gross profit %	24%	30%	
Operating (loss)/profit	£432,000	£300,000	
Operating profit %	12%	15%	
Interest cover	3 times	4 times	
Current ratio	1.68	2.0	
Quick (acid test) ratio	0.8	1.2	
Non-current assets	£1,743,000	£972,000	
Cash in hand and at bank	£0	£38,000	
Bank overdraft/bank loan	£1,501,000	£670,000	
Share capital	£250,000	£250,000	
Reserves	£350,000	£685,300	

The standard terms of trade of Mungojerry Ltd are 30 days.

(a) **Explain overtrading and analyse the application form for extended credit from Rumpleteazer to assess whether the company is overtrading.**

(b) **Using the information provided, recommend whether the request for extended credit terms should be granted. You must justify your decision and indicate any additional information that could be obtained before a final decision is made.**

COLLECTION OF DEBTS

COLLECTION OF DEBTS

113 Which of the following are the costs to a business of granting credit to their customers?

	Tick
Finance charges.	
Increase in irrecoverable debts.	
Increase in liquidity.	
Increase in the amount of administration.	

114 Which of the following are costs of offering credit terms to a customer?

	Tick
Extra administration.	
Increase in irrecoverable debts.	
Increased use of financing.	
Improved short term liquidity.	

115 Which of the following are the benefits to a business of granting credit to their customers?

(i) Reduced finance charges.

(ii) Decrease in irrecoverable debts.

(iii) Increase in liquidity.

(iv) Decrease in the amount of administration.

Options:

A (ii) and (iii) only

B (i), (ii) and (iv) only

C (ii), (iii) and (iv) only

D None of the above

116 Which of the following are benefits of offering a cash discount scheme?

(i) Extra administration.

(ii) Reduction in irrecoverable debts.

(iii) Improved customer relations.

(iv) Improved short term liquidity.

Options:

A (i) (ii) and (iv) only

B (i) and (ii) only

C (ii), (iii) and (iv)

D All of the above

117 When a company is concerned that historically on average 5% of the sales ledger will not pay their debt it should?

A Write off 5% of the ledger as an irrecoverable debt

B Make a specific provision

C Make a general provision of 5% of the sales ledger

D Offer a 5% settlement discount

118 Alpha Limited has sold goods on credit to Beta Limited. The following information is available.

(i) Aged receivable analysis.

(ii) Copies of outstanding invoices.

(iii) Copies of contractual documents.

(iv) Copies of trade references.

(v) Copies of bank references.

Which of the above documents will be needed to aid the collection of the outstanding amounts owed by Beta Limited?

A All items

B (i), (ii) and (iii) only

C (i), (iv) and (v) only

D (iv) and (v) only

119 Customers currently pay 30 days after the month end. A 2% discount is being offered from February if customers settle the invoice in the same month. It is expected that 70% of customers will take advantage of this. The expected sales revenue per month is as follows:

January £50,000

February £75,000

March £90,000

Calculate the expected cash receipts in March.

120 Why is liquidity management important?

A Liquidity management is important to ensure that a company does not make a loss.

B Liquidity management is important so that the shareholders can see how much return they will get on their investment.

C Liquidity management is important so that the company can estimate how much cash is tied up in inventory and non-current assets.

D Liquidity management is important so that the company can ensure that cash is available to discharge commitments.

SETTLEMENT DISCOUNTS

121 Which of the following is a reason for offering discounts for prompt payment?

A To improve the short term cash flow of a business

B To increase the profit on that sale

C To reduce administrative costs

D To increase the receipts from receivables

122 A supplier of computer equipment allows its customers to deduct 3% from the invoice amount if they pay within 14 days of the invoice date.

This is an example of:

A A irrecoverable debt

B A trade discount

C A cash transaction

D A settlement discount

123 Which of the following is a reason for offering discounts for prompt payment?

A To make the customer feel that they have received a bargain

B To improve the cash flow of a business

C To make more profit

D To decrease the cost of loans

124 A company's terms of payment are 28 days. It is offering a discount of 5% for payment within 14 days. Customer A owes £1,000.

Calculate the simple annual interest rate of the discount.

A 137.22%

B 36.84%

C 130%

D 30%

125 A company is offering a cash discount of 2.5% to credit customers if they settle within one month rather than the normal two months (assume 30 days in a month).

What is the simple annual interest rate of the discount?

A 30.0%

B 30.8%

C 31.2%

D 33.5%

126 **What is the simple cost of giving a 4% prompt payment discount to customers who pay within 30 days rather than the usual 90 days?**

A 25%

B 10%

C 21%

D 16%

127 A company is offering a cash discount of 5% to credit customers if they settle within one month rather than the normal four months (assume 30 days in a month).

What is the compound annual interest rate of the discount?

A 23.1%

B 22.0%

C 22.3%

D 22.9%

128 A company's terms of payment are 28 days. It is offering a 4.5% discount for payment within 7 days. Customer X owes £400.

Calculate the amount X will pay if they take advantage of the discount and also the compound annual interest rate of the discount?

A £382 and 81.9%

B £382 and 122.6%

C £360 and 81.9%

D £360 and 122.6%

129 **What is the compound cost of giving a 1% prompt payment discount to customers who pay within 14 days rather than the usual 44 days?**

A 15%

B 12%

C 13%

D 11%

130 The Sales Manager has found that her sales staff do not understand the annual percentage cost of the early settlement discounts that the company offers to customers.

Complete the following sentences:

If a customer pays promptly to take advantage of a 3% early settlement discount, we will receive 97% of the invoice total. This means that the discount we are giving the customer is _______% of the amount they pay us (2 decimal places). This is what it costs us to receive the cash earlier than our normal credit terms. It is the effective rate of interest.

If the normal credit terms require customers to pay within 60 days of receiving an invoice, and the discount applies if the customer pays within 21 days, we are offering the discount in return for paying 39 days earlier than our normal terms. There are _____ discount periods of 39 days in a 365 day year (2 decimal places).

The annual simple percentage cost is found by **multiplying/dividing*** the effective rate of interest and the discount periods in a year. The annual simple percentage cost of offering 3% discount to customers paying within 21 days rather than 60 days is _________ % (to the nearest whole percent).

131 **Current sales revenue is £30,000 a month and currently customers pay 60 days after the month end. In April the company is introducing a 2.5% prompt payment discount to customers who pay within 10 days rather than the usual 60 days. It is expected that 70% of customers will take advantage of the discount. Cash receipts in May will be?**

A £20,475

B £30,000

C £50,475

D £60,000

132 A company's terms of payment are 40 days. It is offering a 5.5% discount for payment within 14 days. Customer X owes £250.

Calculate the amount X will pay if they take advantage of the discount and also the simple annual interest rate of the discount?

A £236.25 and 81.7%

B £236.25 and 61.7%

C £225.75 and 81.7%

D £225.75 and 61.7%

FACTORING, DISCOUNTING AND INSURANCE

133 A company is considering factoring as a way of managing its trade receivables. It currently has a balance outstanding of £250,000. It has annual sales revenue of £1,500,000 which occurs evenly throughout the year. Trade receivables are expected to continue at the same level for the next year.

The factor will advance 80% of invoiced sales and will charge a fee of 10% of all invoiced sales.

The fee for the next year payable to the factor will be:

A £25,000

B £150,000

C £20,000

D £120,000

134 A company is considering the use of without recourse factoring to manage its trade receivables.

It currently has a balance outstanding on trade receivables of £180,000 and annual sales revenue of £1,095,000. It anticipates that this level of sales revenue and trade receivables will continue for at least the next year. It estimates that the use of the factoring company will result in a reduction in credit control costs of £20,000 per annum.

The factoring company will charge a fee of 2.5% of all invoiced sales. It will give an advance of 90% of invoiced sales and charge interest at a rate of 12% per annum.

Calculate the annual cost of factoring net of credit control cost savings?

A £26,815

B £46,815

C £98,260

D £118,260

135 A company is looking to improve its cash flow and has been considering various finance products. The company has a balance on its sales ledger of £1,250,145 as at the 31 July 20X3.

A finance company has offered to provide a facility where the company can borrow up to £750,000 or a maximum of 80% of the total outstanding sales ledger balance. The finance company administers the sales ledger on behalf of the company for a fee of £1,500 per month.

The maximum amount available to borrow at the 31 July 20X3 is:

£

136 **Invoice discounting is a method where:**

A Discounts are given for early payment of invoices

B A finance house lends money against invoices issued

C A reduction is given for faulty goods

D A judgement given by a court

137 Spruce Ltd is considering methods to speed up receipts from credit customers and has been offered a without-recourse factoring arrangement.

Which of the following is NOT likely to be an advantage of such an agreement?

A Insurance against irrecoverable debts

B Improved relationship with customers

C Managers can spend more time running the company rather than credit control

D Reduced overdraft

138 Credit insurance allows a company to claim for:

A Amounts owed by a customer who has defaulted on payment

B Amounts owed to a bank on a mortgage

C Amounts owed to payables when a company makes losses

D Amounts owed to shareholders when a director has acted illegally

139 Which one of the following is not a service typically provided by a debt factoring company?

A Supply of goods to a customer

B Finance

C Administration of the sales ledger

D Credit protection

140 Put the following in the correct order if a business is using a debt factor:

(i) The factor sends cash to the business.

(ii) The customer pays the factoring company.

(iii) The business sends an invoice to the customer.

(iv) The balance on the debt is paid to the business by the factor less any fees owing.

(v) The factoring company chases the outstanding debts.

Options:

A (iii), (i), (v), (ii), (iv)

B (i), (ii), (iii), (iv), (v)

C (v), (ii), (i), (iii), (vi)

D (iii), (iv), (ii), (v), (i)

141 Which of the following is an advantage of Invoice discounting over debt factoring?

A Cash is advanced to the business

B A reduction in the cost of credit control

C The customer deals only with the business it bought the goods/services from

D The customer pays less than invoiced

142 Which of the following are advantages of using a debt factor for collection of debts?

(i) A reduction in credit control costs.

(ii) Improved short term cash flow.

(iii) A reduction in finance charges for the business.

(iv) Improved reputation of the business.

Options:

A (i) and (ii) only

B (i), (ii) and (iii) only

C (ii) and (iv) only

D (ii), (iii) and (iv) only

143 Put the following in the correct order if a business is using Invoice discounter:

(i) The discounter sends cash to the business.

(ii) The customer pays the business.

(iii) The business sends an invoice to the customer.

(iv) The business pays the discounter what was advanced plus fees.

(v) The business chases the outstanding debt.

Options:

A (iii), (i), (v), (ii), (iv)

B (i), (ii), (iii), (iv), (v)

C (v), (ii), (i), (iii), (vi)

D (iii), (iv), (ii), (v), (i)

144 Which one of the following is a service typically provided by an Invoice discounting company?

A Supply of goods to a customer

B Finance

C Administration of the sales ledger

D Credit protection

MANAGING TRADE RECEIVABLES

DEBT COLLECTION PROCEDURES

145 The 80/20 rule method of analysing information on receivables is:

A A rule where you only look at the first 80 customer records

B A rule that 20 customers out of every 100 will go into liquidation

C A rule that approximately 80% of the value of the amounts owed will be represented by approximately 20% of the customer accounts

D A rule that the company must make at least 20% profit out of every £100 of goods sold

146 A possible debt collection policy might involve the following steps:

a Send Statement

b Irrecoverable debt

c Legal action letter

d Issue invoice

e Telephone call

f Customer on stop

g Provision for doubtful debt

h Reminder letter

i Start legal action

A sensible order for the above steps would be:

A d a e f c g i b h

B d e h f c g i b a

C d a c g b i e h f

D d a e h f c g i b

147 Under what circumstances should a business write off an outstanding debt?

A When amounts are 30 days over due

B When there are rumours that a business is having difficulties paying debts

C When bankruptcy has been declared

D When an account is put on stop

148 What is the purpose of an aged receivables analysis?

A To monitor the time receivables are outstanding

B To list irrecoverable debts

C To hold receivables temporarily

D To calculate credit limits

149 Organisations often use debt collection agencies because:

A Debt collection agencies have more powers than ordinary companies.

B Debt collection agencies can place customers on stop with all other suppliers in the sector.

C Debt collection agencies have a right to seize goods from customer.

D Debt collection agencies get results because customers take more notice and are more likely to pay.

150 A regular review of the aged trade receivable analysis should highlight which of the following?

(i) Poor trade references.

(ii) Credit limit exceeded.

(iii) Slow payers.

(iv) Lack of financial statements from the customer.

Options:

A (i) and (ii) only

B (i), (ii) and (iii) only

C (ii) and (iii) only

D All of the above

151 When analysing the trade receivables to assess the level of potential irrecoverable debts which of the following would not be useful to you in this task?

A Correspondence with trade receivables

B Press comment

C Information from the sales team

D Detailed aged payable analysis

152 Which of the following are required if a retention of title claim is to be successful?

	Tick
The goods need to be in the possession of the seller	
Every invoice must show a retention of title clause	
The goods must be easily identifiable	
Goods should be in their original form	

153 A regular review of the aged trade receivable analysis should highlight which of the following?

(i) Poor bank references.

(ii) Credit term exceeded.

(iii) Problem invoices.

(iv) Customers with liquidity problems.

Options:

A (i) and (ii) only

B (i), (ii) and (iii) only

C (ii) and (iii) only

D All of the above

154 Bill has received a letter from the liquidator of Ben Ltd. The liquidator has indicated that all unsecured creditors of Ben will receive a dividend of 3.5p in the pound (£) later in the year. Bill is owed £5,000 by Ben.

Calculate the amount that Bill should write off as an irrecoverable debt (ignore VAT). State your answer to the nearest penny.

£

155 The trade receivable ledger account for customer J from 1 January to 30 April 20X0 shows the following:

		Debit	**Credit**	**Balance**
01 Jan 20X0	B/fwd			125
10 Jan 20X0	Invoice 234	181		306
12 Jan 20X0	Invoice 263	92		398
18 Jan 20X0	Invoice 297	287		685
23 Jan 20X0	Receipt 85 (bal and inv 263)		217	468
09 Feb 20X0	Invoice 328	294		762
13 Feb 20X0	Credit note 167 (Inv 234)		63	699
05 Mar 20X0	Invoice 365	135		834
15 Mar 20X0	Invoice 379	232		1,066
18 Mar 20X0	Receipt 102 (Inv 297)		287	779
25 Mar 20X0	Invoice 391	71		850
01 Apr 20X0	Receipt 126 (Inv 328)		294	556
24 Apr 20X0	Invoice 438	145		701

Prepare an age analysis of trade receivables, for customer J, at 30 April 20X0 showing the outstanding balance analysed by month.

156 You work for KL Limited as Chief Credit Controller.

One of the Credit Controllers has asked your advice in collecting the debt due from one of its customers, Demi Limited. Demi Limited is a large customer and often pays late. The MD of KL Limited is an old school friend of the MD of Demi Limited and the pair often play cricket together.

The amount outstanding is currently £100,000 which is equal to four months of trade. KL has sent a statement for the last two months but has not heard from Demi Limited.

Explain what KL Limited should do to collect the amount owing from Demi Limited.

157 Below is the credit control procedure for Laidback Ltd:

1 Order received by email, fax or phone (all calls are recorded).

2 The Finance manager has 'got a lot of experience in business' and so decides if new customers can be granted credit and how much.

3 Mrs Jones raises the invoices and has a policy of raising invoices on the 1st of the month following sale because she says that as credit policy is 30 days it 'keeps everything tidy'.

4 Aged receivable analysis is produced monthly.

5 When an invoice is 1 month overdue a letter is sent, and 3 weeks later a phone call is made.

6 Every six months a final review of overdue receivables is carried out and receivables over 60 days overdue are put in the hands of a debt collection agency, or legal proceedings are taken.

Outline the weaknesses of the above system, making recommendations of your own.

LEGAL ACTION

158 **What is insolvency?**

A When a company needs to appoint a credit controller

B When a company pays its debts late

C When a company is only able to pay some of its debts as they fall due

D When a company is unable to pay debts as they fall due

159 **Match each type of claim on the left to the appropriate type of court procedure on the right.**

Claim	Court procedure
Over £25,000	Magistrate Court under the Fast Track
	High Court or County Court under the Multi Track route
£10,000 – £25,000	High Court under the Small Claims Track
	County Court under the Fast Track
Under £10,000	County Court under the Small Claims Track

160 In order to petition the court for a winding up order the company must be owed at least:

A £75

B £750

C £7,500

D £1,000

161 DC plc is owed £4,000 by a customer who refuses to pay, despite DC having secured a County Court Judgement against them. DC has gone back to the Court and a court bailiff has been given authority to take goods from the customer's home or business.

What is this arrangement known as?

A A warrant of execution

B An attachment of earnings order

C A garnishee order

D A charging order

162 Once a court order has been made then the money can be collected in a number of ways. A Charging Order is:

A the seizure of goods

B the lawful owner gains a court order that states that items must be returned

C the court can order a charge on the receivable's property and if the debt is not paid within six months the payable has the right to have the property sold

D the payable is paid directly by the receivable's employer out of his/her/their pay packet

163 Once a court order has been made then the money can be collected in a number of ways. A Warrant of Delivery is:

A the seizure of goods

B the lawful owner gains a court order that states that items must be returned

C the court can order a charge on the receivable's property and if the debt is not paid within six months the payable has the right to have the property sold

D the payable is paid directly by the receivable's employer out of his/her/their pay packet

164 What is liquidation?

A A commercial process in which a receiver is appointed to restructure the company

B A legal process in which a liquidator is appointed to wind up the affairs of a limited company

C A civil process in which a director is appointed to liquidate the company

D A legal process to pursue the directors for wrongful trading

165 Which of the following are stages in a company winding up procedure?

	Tick
Bankruptcy order	
Petition to the Court	
Appointment of Administrator	
Statutory demand	

166 For a bankruptcy order to succeed the debt must be:

(i) In excess of £550.

(ii) Unsecured.

(iii) The receivable must live in the UK.

(iv) Owing for a minimum of 6 months.

Options:

A (i), (ii) and (iv) only

B (i) and (ii) only

C (ii) and (iii) only

D All of the above

167 What is the order of distributions once a bankruptcy order has been declared?

(i) Fees and charges of the bankruptcy or liquidation process.

(ii) Unsecured creditors.

(iii) The bankrupt, or company shareholders.

(iv) Floating charge holders (companies only).

(v) Preferential creditors.

(vi) Fixed charge holders.

Options:

A (i), (ii),(iii), (iv), (v), (vi)

B (i), (v), (iv), (ii), (iii), (iv)

C (vi), (i), (iv), (v), (ii), (iii)

D (vi), (i), (v), (iv), (ii), (iii)

168 Which one of the following are true of false for a Company Voluntary Arrangement (CVA)?

	True	False
A CVA is applied where the business has no ongoing future		
A CVA is agreed between the business and creditors		
A CVA is voluntary and hence not legally binding		
At least 75% of creditors must agree to the CVA		
Under a CVA the business will pay back a proportion of the debts owed over a period of time		
The CVA is monitored by the government		

CUSTOMER ANALYSIS

169 You have been provided with the credit control policy for Lamb Limited and an aged receivable's analysis at 31 March 20X2.

Credit control policy for Lamb Limited.

1 Current credit control procedures once credit limit has been agreed:

2 An order for goods is received by email, fax or phone (all phone calls are recorded).

3 Goods are delivered and a goods received note is signed by the customer.

4 The goods received notes are kept in a file in the accounts office.

5 An invoice will be issued a few days after delivery on 30 day terms.

6 An aged analysis of trade receivables is produced monthly.

7 A reminder telephone call is made when the debt is 7 days overdue.

8 When a debt is 14 days overdue a letter is sent.

9 When the account is 28 days overdue the account will be put on stop.

10 The debt will either be placed in the hands of a debt collection company or legal proceedings could be instigated if the customer does not respond to calls or letters.

11 The business is credit insured, however insurance is only given for customers once they have a history of trade with the business of at least 12 months and have successfully paid for at least 3 invoiced amounts.

Aged receivables analysis as at 31 March 20X2

Customer	**Balance** £	**0 – 30 days** £	**31 – 60 days** £	**61 – 90 days** £	**Over 90 days** £
Pink	10,000	10,000			
Blue	25,000			25,000	
Green	60,000	30,000	30,000		
White	35,000	10,000	10,000	15,000	
Brown	60,000	60,000			
Cerise	25,000	5,000	20,000		

Notes provided by the assistant credit controller

(a) Pink is a new customer and placed its first order a few weeks ago.

(b) Blue have said that they placed an order for a particular grade of product but received a different product and are therefore not prepared to pay the invoice.

(c) Green is a new customer and has said that a cheque is in the post. There is a rumour circulating that the company is having financial problems and has not been paying its suppliers. Green has placed an order for £10,000 of goods.

(d) White has a history of paying late but they have always paid eventually.

(e) Brown is a long standing customer and has always settled their account within trading terms.

(f) Cerise has gone into administration. The account is not credit insured.

Complete the table below by selecting from the following list of options:

- A chasing letter should be sent and the account should be on stop. A telephone call maybe needed to discuss credit terms.
- Put the account on stop until payment is received, do not process any more orders. A provision for the outstanding amounts may be provided for.
- Contact the insolvency practitioner to register a claim and a provision should be made in the accounts.
- Check the sales order and delivery note for any error.
- No action needed.

Customer	**Action**
Pink	
Blue	
Green	
White	
Brown	
Cerise	

170 You have been provided with the credit control policy for Pocket Limited and an aged receivables' analysis at 31 March 20X1.

Credit control policy for Pocket Limited

Current credit control procedures once credit limit has been agreed:

1 An order for goods is received by email, fax or phone (all phone calls are recorded).

2 Goods are delivered and a goods received note is signed by the customer.

3 The goods received notes are kept in a file in the accounts office.

4 An invoice will be issued a few days after delivery on 30 day terms.

5 An aged analysis of trade receivables is produced monthly.

6 A reminder telephone call is made when the debt is 7 days overdue.

7 When a debt is 14 days overdue a letter is sent.

8 When the account is 28 days overdue the account will be put on stop.

9 The debt will either be placed in the hands of a debt collection company or legal proceedings could be instigated if the customer does not respond to calls or letters.

10 The business is credit insured, however insurance is only given for customers once they have a history of trade with the business of at least 12 months and have successfully paid for at least 3 invoiced amounts. Only 80% of the value of the debt is insured. VAT will be reclaimed from HMRC.

11 Pocket Limited has a retention of title clause in the contract.

Aged receivable analysis as at 31 March 20X1

Customer	**Balance** £	**0–30 days** £	**31–60 days** £	**61–90 days** £	**Over 90 days** £
Bag Limited	12,000	12,000			
Sack Limited	27,000	7,000	20,000		
Basket Limited	12,000	(50,000)	12,000		50,000
Barrow Limited	128,000	32,000	32,000	32,000	32,000
Box Limited	120,000			120,000	
Satchel	27,000			27,000	

Notes provided by the assistant credit controller

(a) Bag Limited is a new customer and placed its first order a few weeks ago. The goods were delivered on 16 March and the invoice was raised on 17 March on 30 day terms.

(b) Sack Limited has gone into liquidation. The account is not credit insured.

(c) Basket Limited sent a payment of £50,000 but did not provide details of which invoices the payment relates to.

(d) Barrow Limited is a long established customer and has always paid eventually, but has a history of late payments. Unallocated cash of £64,000 has been traced to a receipt from Barrow Limited. Barrow Limited has confirmed that the payment is for the two older invoices.

(e) Box Limited has recently gone into liquidation. Box Limited had been a customer for 5 years and the account is credit insured.

(f) Satchel's 61–90 day balance is one invoice dated 15 January. Satchel has requested proof of delivery.

Select the correct course of action for each customer

(a) Bag Limited

A The account is overdue and a phone call should have been made on 24 March and a letter sent on 31 March.

B The account is not overdue so no action is required.

C The account should be put on stop.

(b) Sack Limited

A Contact the insolvency practitioner and a provision should only be made after the debt is more than six months old.

B Sack Limited's offices should be visited to identify the goods and register a retention of title claim with the insolvency service.

C Sack Limited's offices should be visited to identify the goods and register a retention of title claim with the insolvency practitioner.

D The insolvency service should be contacted to register the claim and a provision should be made in the accounts.

(c) Basket Limited

A Basket Limited should be put on hold until the dispute is resolved.

B Basket Limited should be contacted to confirm which invoices are being paid so the unallocated receipt can be allocated.

C The £50,000 should be returned to Basket Limited.

D The £50,000 should be allocated to the last invoice first.

(d) Barrow Limited

A The unallocated cash needs to be adjusted by debiting the unallocated cash by £64,000 and crediting Barrow Limited accounts by £64,000.

B The unallocated cash needs to be adjusted by crediting the unallocated cash by £64,000 and debiting Barrow Limited accounts by £64,000.

C The unallocated cash needs to be adjusted by debiting the unallocated cash by £64,000 and debiting Barrow Limited accounts by £64,000.

D The unallocated cash needs to be adjusted by crediting the unallocated cash by £64,000 and crediting Barrow Limited accounts by £64,000.

(e) Box Limited

A Credit Insurance (CI) claim will be made for £100,000 and VAT of £20,000 will be reclaimed from HMRC.

B CI claim will be made for £96,000; a provision needs to be made for £24,000.

C CI claim will be made for £80,000; a provision needs to be made for £20,000 and VAT of £20,000 will be reclaimed from HMRC.

D CI claim will be made for £67,200; a provision needs to be made for £28,800 and VAT of £24,000 will be reclaimed from HMRC.

E CI claim will be made for £96,000 and VAT of £24,000 will be reclaimed from HMRC.

(f) Satchel

A Send the original delivery note which was signed by Satchel.

B Send a copy of the delivery note which was signed by Satchel.

C Instruct a debt collection company to collect the debt.

171 You have been provided with the credit control policy for Hardy Limited. Today's date is 31 March 20X1.

Credit control policy for Hardy Limited

Current credit control procedures once credit limit has been agreed:

1 An order for goods is received by email, fax or phone (all phone calls are recorded).

2 Goods are delivered and a goods received note is signed by the customer.

3 The goods received notes are kept in a file in the accounts office.

4 An invoice will be issued a few days after delivery on 30 day terms.

5 An aged analysis of trade receivables is produced monthly.

6 A reminder telephone call is made when the debt is 7 days overdue.

7 When a debt is 14 days overdue a letter is sent.

8 When the account is 28 days overdue the account will be put on stop.

9 The debt will either be placed in the hands of a debt collection company or legal proceedings could be instigated if the customer does not respond to calls or letters.

10 The business is credit insured, however insurance is only given for customers once they have a history of trade with the business of at least 12 months and have successfully paid for at least 3 invoiced amounts. Only 75% of the value of the debt is insured. VAT is reclaimed from HMRC.

Identify the best course of action for each of the following customers

(a) The balance on Mutley's account is £10,000. This consists of two invoices, one for £7,500 which is not overdue, one for £2,500 which is overdue. An unallocated payment has been received for £2,500 and posted to the unallocated payment accounts in the purchase ledger. It has not been identified as a receipt from Mutley.

A Debit Mutley's account and credit unallocated payments with £2,500.

B Credit Mutley's account and debit unallocated payments with £2,500.

C Debit Mutley's account and credit unallocated payments with £7,500.

D Credit Mutley's account and debit unallocated payments with £7,500.

(b) Dastardly has a balance of £30,000 is 68 days overdue and is for one invoice. Dastardly claims that the goods were not received.

A Send the original delivery note signed by Dastardly.

B Raise a credit note for £30,000.

C Send a copy of the signed delivery note which was signed by Dastardly.

D Send a copy of the signed delivery note signed by the courier who delivered the goods.

(c) Mouse is a new customer and has said that a cheque for the outstanding amount of £15,000 is in the post. There is a rumour circulating that the company is having financial problems and has not been paying its suppliers. Mouse has placed a further order for £25,000 of goods.

A Allow further order and wait for the cheque to appear.

B Do not allow further order and wait for the cheque to appear.

C Put the account on stop and make a provision for the outstanding amount.

D Start legal proceedings.

(d) Pan sent a payment of £50,000 but did not provide details of which invoices the payment relates to.

A Pan should be contacted to confirm which invoices are being paid so that the unallocated receipts can be allocated.

B The £50,000 should be returned to Pan.

C The £50,000 should be allocated to the last invoices first.

D The £50,000 should be posted to unallocated payments.

(e) Beagly has gone into administration after being a customer for three years. Up until five months ago they had always paid to terms.

A Contact the insolvency service and register a claim with the credit insurer.

B Contact the insolvency practitioner and register a claim with the credit insurer.

C Place the account on stop and contact a debt collection company to deal with processing a claim against Beagly.

D Visit the premises of Beagly and seize goods to the value of the outstanding balance.

172 You have been provided with the credit control policy for Workstation Limited. Today's date is 31 March 20X1.

Credit control policy for Workstation Limited.

Current credit control procedures once credit limit has been agreed:

1 An order for goods is received by email, fax or phone (all phone calls are recorded).

2 Goods are delivered and a goods received note is signed by the customer.

3 The goods received notes are kept in a file in the accounts office.

4 An invoice will be issued two days after delivery on 30 day terms.

5 An aged analysis of trade receivables is produced monthly.

6 A reminder telephone call is made when the debt is 14 days overdue.

7 When a debt is 21 days overdue a letter is sent.

8 When the account is 35 days overdue the account will be put on stop.

9 The debt will either be placed in the hands of a debt collection company or legal proceedings could be instigated if the customer does not respond to calls or letters.

10 The business is credit insured, however insurance is only given for customers once they have a history of trade with the business of at least 12 months and have successfully paid for at least 3 invoiced amounts. 70% of the value of the debt is insured. VAT can be reclaimed from HMRC.

Identify the best course of action for each of the following customers

(a) Chest Limited is a new customer and has said that the goods were not received. There is a balance of £5,000 that is 50 days overdue.

A Send the original delivery note signed by the customer.

B Send a copy of the delivery note signed by the customer.

C Raise a credit note for £5,000.

D Send a copy of the delivery note signed by the courier that delivered the goods.

(b) Stool Limited has gone into administration after being a customer for 6 years. Up until 4 months ago they had been paying to terms.

A Place the account on stop and contact a debt collection agency to deal with processing a claim against Stool Limited.

B Visit the premises and seize goods up to the value of the outstanding balance.

C Contact the insolvency service and register a claim with the credit insurer.

D Contact the insolvency practitioner and register a claim with the credit insurer.

(c) Bookcase Trader owes £27,000 (VAT inclusive) and is refusing to pay even though there is no dispute. The account is on stop. Attempts to contact the customer by letter and telephone have been unsuccessful. The account is credit insured.

Complete the sentences:

Contact the credit insurer and claim £________

Make a provision for £_____

Claim VAT of £______

(d) Shelf Limited sent a payment of £32,000 but did not provide details of which invoices the payment relates to.

A Shelf should be contacted to confirm which invoices the payment relates to.

B The £32,000 should be sent back to the customer.

C The £32,000 should be allocated to the most recent invoice first.

D The £32,000 should be posted to unallocated payments.

(e) The balance on Bed Limited's account is £67,300. This consists of two invoices, one for £30,000 which is not overdue and one for £13,000 which is overdue. An unallocated payment has been received for £13,000 and posted to the unallocated payment accounts in the purchase ledger. It has now been identified as a receipt from Bed Limited.

The action needed is to:

A Debit the unallocated cash by £13,000 and credit the customer's account by £13,000.

B Credit the unallocated cash by £13,000 and debit the customer's account by £13,000.

C Debit the unallocated cash by £13,000 and debit the customer's account by £13,000.

D Credit the unallocated cash by £13,000 and credit the customer's account by £13,000.

(f) Bath Trader is a new customer and placed its first order a few weeks ago. The goods were delivered on 16 March and the invoice was raised on 17 March on 30 day terms.

A The account is overdue and a phone call should have been made on 24 March and a letter sent on 31 March.

B The account is not overdue so no action is required.

C The account should be put on stop.

173 You have been provided with the credit control policy for Rooney Limited and an aged receivables' analysis at 30 April 20X1.

Credit control policy for Rooney Limited.

Current credit control procedures once credit limit has been agreed:

1 An order for goods is received by email, fax or phone (all phone calls are recorded).

2 Goods are delivered and a goods received note is signed by the customer.

3 The goods received notes are kept in a file in the accounts office.

4 An invoice will be issued 4 days after delivery on 30 day terms.

5 An aged analysis of trade receivables is produced monthly.

6 A reminder telephone call is made when the debt is 7 days overdue.

7 When a debt is 14 days overdue a letter is sent.

8 When the account is 28 days overdue the account will be put on stop.

9 The debt will either be placed in the hands of a debt collection company or legal proceedings could be instigated if the customer does not respond to calls or letters.

10 The business is credit insured, however insurance is only given for customers once they have a history of trade with the business of at least 12 months and have successfully paid for at least 3 invoiced amounts. 90% of the debt is insured and VAT will be reclaimed from HMRC.

11 Rooney Limited has a retention of title clause in the contract.

Aged receivable analysis as at 30 April 20X1

Customer	**Balance** £	**0–30 days** £	**31–60 days** £	**61–90 days** £	**Over 90 days** £
Atkinson Trader	25,000		25,000		
Coppell Limited	2,000	(13,000)	5,000	10,000	
Beardsmore Trader	4,000		4,000		
McGrath Limited	7,000		7,000		
Olson Limited	30,000			17,000	13,000
Davenport Trader	3,000			3,000	

Notes provided by the assistant credit controller

(a) Atkinson Limited is a new customer and placed its first order a few weeks ago. The goods were delivered on 7 March and the invoice was raised on 11 March on 30 days terms.

(b) Coppell Limited made an electronic payment into our bank account but didn't provide details as to what the payment related to.

(c) Beardsmore Trader. This amount relates to 20 items that were ordered and came to a total of £4,000. Beardsmore is refusing to pay though as one of the items is different from that ordered.

(d) McGrath Limited. When we have tried to contact them by phone the message says 'number out of service' and our reminder letter was returned to us 'not known at this address'. They are a new customer.

(e) Olson Limited has just gone into liquidation, they have been a customer for the last 3 years and their account is credit insured.

(f) Davenport Trader is an individual customer who is refusing to pay even though there is no dispute.

Select the correct option for each customer.

Customer	**Action**	**Tick correct option**
Atkinson Limited	The account is overdue and a phone call should have been made on 18 April and a letter sent on 25 April.	
	The account is not overdue so no action is required.	
	The account should be on stop.	
Coppell Limited	Coppell Limited should be put on hold until the dispute is resolved.	
	Coppell Limited should be contacted to confirm which invoices are being paid so the unallocated receipt can be allocated.	
	The £13,000 should be returned to Coppell Limited.	
	The £13,000 should be allocated to the last invoice first.	
Beardsmore Trader	Arrange for redelivery of the order.	
	Request payment of debt in full.	
	Put the account on stop.	
	Request payment for the 19 correct items and if no payment is forthcoming contact the debt collection company.	
McGrath Limited	A provision should be made for the debt. Credit insurance is not valid.	
	A claim should be made with the insurance company.	
	Legal proceedings should be commenced.	
	The account should be put on stop.	

Olson Limited	Credit Insurance (CI) claim will be made for £25,000 and VAT of £5,000 will be reclaimed from HMRC.	
	CI claim will be made for £22,500; a provision needs to be made for £2,500 and VAT of £5,000 will be reclaimed from HMRC.	
	CI claim will be made for £24,000 and VAT of £6,000 will be reclaimed from HMRC.	
	CI claim will be made for £21,600; a provision needs to be made for £2,400 and VAT of £6,000 will be reclaimed from HMRC.	
	CI claim will be made for £27,000; a provision needs to be made for £3,000.	
Davenport Trader	Legal proceedings should be started. A provision should be made.	
	A telephone call should be made to chase the debt.	
	A letter should be sent.	
	The account should be put on stop.	

174 You have been provided with the credit control policy for Duran Limited and an aged receivables' analysis at 30 September 20X1.

Credit control policy for Duran Limited.

Current credit control procedures once credit limit has been agreed:

1 An order for goods is received by email, fax or phone (all phone calls are recorded).

2 Goods are delivered and a goods received note is signed by the customer.

3 The goods received notes are kept in a file in the accounts office.

4 An invoice will be issued a few days after delivery on 30 day terms.

5 There is a 2% early settlement discount if payment is made within 14 days of invoice issue date.

6 An aged analysis of trade receivables is produced monthly.

7 A reminder telephone call is made when the debt is 7 days overdue.

8 When a debt is 14 days overdue a letter is sent.

9 When the account is 28 days overdue the account will be put on stop.

10 The debt will either be placed in the hands of a debt collection company or legal proceedings could be instigated if the customer does not respond to calls or letters.

11 The business is credit insured, however insurance is only given for customers once they have a history of trade with the business of at least 12 months and have successfully paid for at least 3 invoiced amounts.

Aged receivable analysis as at 30 September 20X1

Customer	**Balance** £	**0–30 days** £	**31–60 days** £	**61–90 days** £	**Over 90 days** £
Collins Limited	17,000		10,000	7,000	
John Limited	2,000				2,000
Culture Trader	3,000		3,000		
Status Limited	12,000		12,000		
Genesis Limited	62,000		30,000	32,000	
Roxy Limited	30,000	15,000		15,000	

Identify the best course of action for each of the following customers.

(a) Collins Limited has just gone into administration, they have been a customer for the last 3 years and their account is credit insured.

A Contact the insolvency service and register a claim with the credit insurer.

B Place the account on stop and contact a debt collection agency to deal with processing a claim against Stool Limited.

C Visit the premises and seize goods up to the value of the outstanding balance.

D Contact the insolvency practitioner and register a claim with the credit insurer.

(b) John Limited. This amount is outstanding because John Limited paid the amount less the 2% early settlement discount; however the payment was not made in the qualifying period (14 days after invoice issued).

A John Limited should be on hold until the dispute is resolved.

B Make a provision for the outstanding amount.

C Contact John Limited, explain the terms and conditions of the discount. Ask for full payment of the outstanding amount.

D Write off the debt as a gesture of goodwill.

(c) Culture Trader says that their cheque book has been destroyed in a flood so they are awaiting a replacement before paying.

A Wait for payment.

B Ask them to make an electronic (BACS) payment into our account.

C Put the debt in the hands of the debt collection company.

D Start legal proceedings.

(d) Status Limited have said that they cannot pay at the moment as they are in the middle of an audit. The invoice was dated 23rd August. What stage in the credit control procedure should this debt be at?

A Make a reminder phone call.

B Send a reminder letter.

C Put the account on stop.

D Put the debt in the hands of the debt collection company.

E Start legal proceedings.

(e) Genesis Limited is a long established customer and has always paid eventually, but has a history of late payments. The Managing Director of Genesis Limited is a personal friend of Duran Limited's Managing Director.

A Put the account on stop.

B Ask the Managing Director to intervene and call his/her/their contact.

C Do nothing they always pay in the end.

D Start legal action with regards the older invoice.

(f) Roxy Limited has a history of paying late but they have always paid eventually.

A Do nothing they always pay in the end.

B Send a reminder letter.

C Put the account on stop.

D Start legal action with regards the older invoice.

175 Debt collection policy for Piaffe Ltd is as follows:

- Invoices are issued at time of delivery.
- Statements are sent monthly.
- Terms are payment within 30 days.
- Aged analysis is produced monthly.
- Reminder letter is sent when debt is 14 days overdue.
- At 28 days overdue a telephone call is made and account is put on stop.
- At 60 days overdue it is placed in hands of debt collector unless debt is disputed.
- At 90 days overdue legal proceedings are started.

Aged analysis of receivables at 31 March 20X2

Customer	**Balance** £	**Current** £	**31–60 days** £	**61–90 days** £	**Over 90 days** £
Passage Ltd	32,000				32,000
Vault Ltd	24,800		24,800		
Circle Ltd	144,000			48,000	96,000

Notes:

(i) Passage Ltd went into liquidation a little while ago and the statement of affairs shows that there are very few assets.

(ii) Vault Ltd is a regular customer and the latest invoice is dated 28th January 20X2.

(iii) Circle Ltd has historically been a good payer, but there are rumours that the business is currently in trouble due to overtrading.

For each of the above, state what action should have been taken to date, and what further action will be taken? State whether any provision should be made in each case.

176 You have been provided with the credit control policy for Pocket Limited and an aged receivables' analysis at 31 March 20X1.

Credit control policy for Pocket Limited

Current credit control procedures once credit limit has been agreed:

1 An order for goods is received by email, fax or phone (all phone calls are recorded).

2 Goods are delivered and a goods received note is signed by the customer.

3 The goods received notes are kept in a file in the accounts office.

4 An invoice will be issued a few days after delivery on 30 day terms.

5 An aged analysis of trade receivables is produced monthly.

6 A reminder telephone call is made when the debt is 7 days overdue.

7 When a debt is 14 days overdue a letter is sent.

8 When the account is 28 days overdue the account will be put on stop.

9 The debt will either be placed in the hands of a debt collection company or legal proceedings could be instigated if the customer does not respond to calls or letters.

10 The business is credit insured, however insurance is only given for customers once they have a history of trade with the business of at least 12 months and have successfully paid for at least 3 invoiced amounts. Only 80% of the value of the debt is insured. VAT will be reclaimed from HMRC.

11 Pocket Limited has a retention of title clause in the contract.

Customer	**Balance** £	**0–30 days** £	**31–60 days** £	**61–90 days** £	**Over 90 days** £
Case Limited	62,000	31,000	31,000		
Holdall Limited	37,000	10,000	10,000	17,000	
Cart Limited	22,000			22,000	
Trolley Limited	27,000				27,000
Trug Limited	99,400		44,400	55,000	
Tub trader	7,000			7,000	

Notes provided by the assistant credit controller

(a) Case Limited is a new customer and has said that a cheque is in the post. There is a rumour circulating that the company is having financial problems and has not been paying its suppliers. Case Limited has placed an order for £10,000 of goods.

(b) Holdall Limited has a history of paying late but they have always paid eventually.

(c) Cart Limited is a new business and traded on cash with order. The assistant credit controller allowed the order to be processed before the cheque had cleared. The cheque subsequently bounced and the company is not returning calls.

(d) Trolley Limited is a new customer and has said that the goods were not received in good condition. The delivery note states that any claim for poor quality goods has to be notified to Pocket Limited within 24 hours. Trolley Limited only raised a problem with the goods when they were called for the second time. They did not mention that the goods were poor quality on the first call or within 24 hours of delivery.

(e) Trug Limited is a regular customer and normally pays to terms.

(f) Tub trader keeps saying that the cheque is in the post.

Required:

Review the aged receivable analysis and the assistant's notes and prepare an action plan. The action plan should include a summary of options available for the company to pursue and recommendations for provisions or write offs of irrecoverable debts where appropriate.

177 You have been provided with the credit control policy for Lamb Limited and an aged receivable's analysis at 31 March 20X2.

Credit control policy for Lamb Limited.

Current credit control procedures once credit limit has been agreed:

1 An order for goods is received by email, fax or phone (all phone calls are recorded).

2 Goods are delivered and a goods received note is signed by the customer.

3 The goods received notes are kept in a file in the accounts office.

4 An invoice will be issued a few days after delivery on 30 day terms.

5 An aged analysis of trade receivables is produced monthly.

6 A reminder telephone call is made when the debt is 7 days overdue.

7 When a debt is 14 days overdue a letter is sent.

8 When the account is 28 days overdue the account will be put on stop.

9 The debt will either be placed in the hands of a debt collection company or legal proceedings could be instigated if the customer does not respond to calls or letters.

10 The business is credit insured, however insurance is only given for customers once they have a history of trade with the business of at least 12 months and have successfully paid for at least 3 invoiced amounts.

Aged receivables analysis as at 31 March 20X2

Customer	**Balance** £	**0 – 30 days** £	**31 – 60 days** £	**61 – 90 days** £	**Over 90 days** £
Red	10,000	(50,000)	10,000		50,000
Yellow	25,000				25,000
Violet	33,000	33,000			
Amber	20,000			20,000	
Mauve	120,000	30,000	30,000	30,000	30,000
Beige	40,000	20,000	20,000		
Taupe	99,200		44,200	55,000	
Auburn	100,000			100,000	

Notes provided by the assistant credit controller

(a) Red sent a payment of £50,000 but did not provide details of which invoices the payment relates to.

(b) Yellow is a new customer and has said that the goods were not received in good condition. The delivery note states that any claim for poor quality goods has to be notified to Lamb Limited within 24 hours. Yellow only raised a problem with the goods when they were called for the second time. They did not mention that the goods were poor quality on the first call or within 24 hours of delivery.

(c) Violet is a new customer and has only placed the one order. They have not responded to any correspondence and the letter was returned stating the company had gone away.

(d) Amber is a new business and traded on cash with order. The assistant credit controller allowed the order to be processed before the cheque had cleared. The cheque subsequently bounced and the company is not returning calls.

(e) Mauve is a long established customer and has always paid eventually, but has a history of late payments. The Managing Director of Mauve is a personal friend of Lamb Limited's Managing Director.

(f) Beige has been purchasing £20,000 per month. The credit limit is £40,000.

(g) Taupe is a regular customer and normally pays but payment can take several months – usually once a notice of intention to start legal proceedings in issued.

(h) Auburn has recently gone into liquidation. Auburn had been a customer for 5 years and the account is credit insured.

Required:

Review the aged trade receivables analysis and the assistant's notes and prepare an action plan. The action plan should include a summary of options available for the company to pursue and recommendations for provisions or write off of irrecoverable debts where appropriate.

178 Workstation Limited provides goods to the manufacturing sector. Each product is stamped with a batch number so that can be identified. Standard terms and conditions are printed on the back of every invoice, which includes a retention of title clause that states that problems with goods must be notified to Workstation limited within 24 hours of delivery. Any goods that are returned are subject to an administration charge of 5%.

Today's date is 31 March 20X1.

The senior credit controller has asked you to put together notes on some customer accounts.

Credit control policy for Workstation Limited

Current credit control procedures once credit limit has been agreed:

1 An order for goods is received by email, fax or phone (all phone calls are recorded).

2 Goods are delivered and a goods received note is signed by the customer.

3 The goods received notes are kept in a file in the accounts office.

4 An invoice will be issued a few days after delivery on 30 day terms.

5 An aged analysis of trade receivables is produced monthly.

6 A reminder telephone call is made when the debt is 7 days overdue.

7 When a debt is 14 days overdue a letter is sent.

8 When the account is 28 days overdue the account will be put on stop.

9 The debt will either be placed in the hands of a debt collection company or legal proceedings could be instigated if the customer does not respond to calls or letters.

10 The business is credit insured, however insurance is only given for customers once they have a history of trade with the business of at least 12 months and have successfully paid for at least 3 invoiced amounts. Only 75% of the value of the debt is insured.

11 All sales invoices include VAT at the standard rate of 20% and VAT is reclaimed from HMRC.

(a) Review the information provided for each of the three customers below and prepare an action plan for collecting the amounts due. Your action plan should include a summary of the options available for the company to pursue and recommendations for provisions or write offs of irrecoverable debts where appropriate.

(i) Wardrobe Limited are refusing to pay an invoice for £54,000 from January claiming that they placed an order for a particular grade of product but received the wrong grade. Wardrobe has asked for the correct grade to be delivered and the wrong grade removed.

(ii) Table Limited has gone into receivership owing £36,000 including VAT at 20%. The receiver has been contacted, who states that it is unlikely that the retention of title will be valid because the company purchased similar items from several suppliers and therefore the goods are not identifiable as being supplied by Workstation Limited. The receiver also stated that the existing debt will be classed as an unsecured creditor of Workstations.

(iii) Bureau Limited is a new customer and has only placed the one order. They have not responded to any correspondence and the invoice was returned stating the company had gone away.

(b) Trunk's account has become corrupt on the system.

Balance at 1 March £12,000

Invoices raised:

5 March £6,500 (VAT inclusive)

12 April £10,500 plus VAT of 20%

Credit notes raised:

15 March £1,500 (VAT inclusive) (subject to restocking fee)

Bank receipts:

20 March £10,000

23 April £15,000

What is the balance on Trunk's account at the end of March and the end of April?

179 Rooney supplies raw material to several customers who then manufacture the materials into finished products. The terms of trade include a clause that errors in delivery must be notified to Rooney with 72 hours of delivery. Rooney has a retention of title clause on some contracts for sale and some customer accounts are credit insured.

You have been provided with the following information from the credit control department of Rooney.

Customer	**Details**
Whiteside Limited	Whiteside Limited has gone into liquidation owing £420,000 plus VAT. A salesman from Rooney visited the premises to attempt to identify the goods. He discovered that 50,000 kilograms were in the raw material state and another 25,000 had been manufactured into finished goods by combining with another material and heat treating. Rooney believes that they have a valid ROT claim and the account is credit insured for 80% of the VAT exclusive amount. The raw materials were specifically formulated for Whiteside Limited and have a scrap value of £1 per kilogram. The receiver has offered to purchase the materials for £3 per kilogram and the original sales price is £7 per kilogram.
Hughes Limited	Hughes Limited is a new customer and has placed one order for £30,000. The amount was due for payments 7 days ago and when contacted Hughes said that a cheque is in the post. Hughes Limited has placed another order for £20,000 of goods and is asking if they can collect the goods in the next few days. Hughes Limited has an agreed credit limit of £60,000.

Martin Limited	Martin Limited's account has become corrupted due to a computer problem. The following information has been recovered. Balance as at 1 May = £5,800. Invoices raised – 12 May £5,000 plus VAT at 20%. 10 June £7,500 plus VAT. Goods returned – 20 May 1,500 kilograms at £3 per kilogram VAT exclusive. Charge for restocking fee – 10% of the cost per kilogram plus VAT. Cash payment received – £3,200 on 25th May, £8,400 on 17 June.
Bailey Limited	Bailey Limited is a new business and has just gone into receivership. The receiver wishes to trade with Rooney for the supply of goods which are needed to manufacture Bailey Limited's products. There are 3,000 kilograms of product in Bailey's warehouse which were delivered prior to the receivership. The invoiced cost of the 3,000 kilograms is £15,000. The receiver has offered £10,000 for the goods and wishes to order a further 5,000 kilograms and has offered £4 per kilogram. The account is not credit insured. The raw material can be purchased from many suppliers and Rooney currently has surplus inventory levels which, if they have to scrap, will only have a value of £2.50 per kilogram.
Gidman Limited	Gidman Limited has said that they placed an order for a particular grade of product, Z23, but received the wrong grade, X23. Gidman has asked if they can have the correct grade delivered and X23 collected. The original invoice is for 1,200 kilograms of product X23 at a cost per kilogram of £14. Material Z23 costs £18 per kilogram. Gidman has asked if they can have product Z23 for the same price as X23 as the mistake was not theirs. Gidman did notify Rooney of the error within 72 hours.

Review the information for each customer and prepare comments and an action plan. The action plan should include a summary of options available for the company to pursue outstanding amounts and recommendations for provisions or write offs of irrecoverable debts where appropriate. Calculate the outstanding balance for Martin Limited at the end of May and June.

180 You have been provided with the credit control policy for Duran Limited and an aged receivables' analysis at 30 September 20X1.

Credit control policy for Duran Limited

Current credit control procedures once credit limit has been agreed:

1 An order for goods is received by email, fax or phone (all phone calls are recorded).

2 Goods are delivered and a goods received note is signed by the customer.

3 The goods received notes are kept in a file in the accounts office.

4 An invoice will be issued a few days after delivery on 30 day terms.

5 There is a 2% early settlement discount if payment is made within 14 days of invoice issue date.

6 An aged analysis of trade receivables is produced monthly.

7 A reminder telephone call is made when the debt is 7 days overdue.

8 When a debt is 14 days overdue a letter is sent.

9 When the account is 28 days overdue the account will be put on stop.

10 The debt will either be placed in the hands of a debt collection company or legal proceedings could be instigated if the customer does not respond to calls or letters.

11 The business is credit insured, however insurance is only given for customers once they have a history of trade with the business of at least 12 months and have successfully paid for at least 3 invoiced amounts.

Aged receivable analysis as at 30 September 20X1

Customer	**Balance** £	**0–30 days** £	**31–60 days** £	**61–90 days** £	**Over 90 days** £
Wham Limited	21,000			21,000	
Spandau Trader	25,000				25,000
Jackson Limited	7,500	7,500			
FYC Limited	10,000		10,000		
Sting Trader	44,000				44,000
Simple Limited	33,000				33,000
Blue Trader	16,000			16,000	
Hardcastle Trader	25,000	25,000			

Notes provided by the assistant credit controller

(a) Wham Limited are disputing an invoice because the price does not reflect a discount that was promised by the salesman. Accounts were not aware of this discount.

(b) Spandau Trader have said that they can't pay their debt at the moment as their customers haven't paid them.

(c) FYC Limited are disputing an item that was out of stock, we sent them a better item as replacement but still charged them the lower price – they want the original item.

(d) Sting Trader. The owner claims to have been ill and resents the 'aggressive persistence' of staff chasing the outstanding amount.

(e) Blue Trader is an individual customer who is refusing to pay even though there is no dispute.

(f) Hardcastle Trader is an individual; you have recently been notified by Interpol that he/she/they is wanted in connection with money laundering.

Required:

Review the aged receivable analysis and the assistant's notes and prepare an action plan. The action plan should include a summary of options available for the company to pursue and recommendations for provisions or write offs of irrecoverable debts where appropriate.

Section 2

ANSWERS TO PRACTICE QUESTIONS

LEGISLATION

CONTRACT LAW FEATURES

1

	True	False
A contract made by a company must be in writing.		✓
A contract of employment must be in writing.		✓

Companies can make oral contracts as well as written ones. An employment contract can also be oral, however, a written statement must be provided to the employee within two months of the commencement of employment.

2 C

This is not an acceptance (or a rejection), purely asking for additional information.

3

	True	False
A promise to perform an existing statutory duty is sufficient to amount to good consideration.		✓
A peppercorn is sufficient to amount to good consideration.	✓	
Past consideration is sufficient to amount to good consideration.		✓

The promise to perform an existing duty cannot amount to consideration. Past consideration is also insufficient. A peppercorn can amount to consideration as it has some value. It is not necessary for the consideration to be adequate (i.e. of equal value).

4 B

The promise to pay in 30 days constitutes consideration.

5

	True	False
A person who signs a contract is deemed to have read it.	✓	
A person who signs a contract is bound by all its terms.		✓
A person who has not read a contract cannot be bound by it.		✓

We are not always bound by all the terms of a contract. For example, under the Unfair Terms in Consumer Contracts Regulations 1999, a consumer is not bound by unintelligible terms.

6 B

7 B

Consideration need not be adequate, but must be sufficient.

8 B

A contract entered into as a result of misrepresentation (fraudulent, negligent or innocent) is voidable.

9 A

Simple contracts can be oral or written. However, for a simple contract to exist there must be agreement (offer and acceptance, consideration and an intention to create legal relations).

10 C

11 D

12 C

13

	Tick
Offer.	✓
Consideration.	✓
Acceptance.	✓
Intention to create legal relations.	✓
Invitation to treat.	

Invitation to treat is not a feature of a simple contract; it is an invitation to the other party in a contract to make an offer (e.g. an advertisement).

14 C

15 A

16 D

17 A

Simple contracts can be oral or written. However, for a simple contract to exist there must be offer and acceptance, capacity, consideration and an intention to create legal relations.

18 C

19 A

CONTRACT LAW APPLICATION

20 D

21 B

The advert in the window is an invitation to treat. When Yasmin makes an offer to buy the phone for £199, S can simply refuse the offer.

22 A

Same principle as in question 21 above.

23 A

Y gave consideration on Saturday when he/she/they made his/her/their promise of payment. If he/she/they fails to pay at the end of the month he/she/they commits a breach of contract.

24 B

The basic principle of contract law is that if you choose to agree by contract to do something then you must do it: if you do it then you get your money; if you don't do it then you're in breach of contract – straightforward and simple! So option B is the application of this basic principle to these facts.

25 D

A fine is a type of punishment and remedies for breach of contract are not meant to punish.

26 D

27 B

28 C

For a contract to exist there must be offer and acceptance, so Answers A and B are both incorrect, even though Answer B might seem a logical position. Answer D is clearly incorrect, since payment in advance is not a required condition for consideration in a contract. Since there has not yet been acceptance by either party, Kai is in a position to withdraw his offer and can also refuse the offer by Emily.

29 **B**

30 **D**

The statement that the television will receive digital channels will be a misrepresentation if it is false as it is a statement of fact. All of the other statements are opinions.

31 **C**

32 **B**

33 **B**

34 **D**

35 **D**

36 **D**

37 **C**

(60 – 45) × £500 = £7,500. Although only 55 days of support has been provided, RTC can charge for the minimum 60 days agreed per the contract.

CONTRACT LAW REMEDIES

38 £4,800 × 9.5% × 50 ÷ 365 = **£62.46.** INTEREST RATE IS 8% PLUS BASE RATE. ROUND DOWN TO NEAREST PENNY

39 **B**

40 **A**

Where goods are sold in the course of a business, Consumer Rights Act implies a condition into the contract that the goods are of satisfactory quality. Knowledge, negligence or fault of the seller is immaterial.

41 **C**

42 **A**

43 **A**

44

	True	False
The hotel is double-booked.		✓
The hotel is struck by lightning and burns down.	✓	
The authorities order the closure of the hotel because of non-compliance with safety regulations.		✓

45 C

Option (iii) correctly describes the compensatory purpose of damages. The purpose is not to punish either party.

46 C

Regarding option (iii), very exceptionally damages are awarded for loss of enjoyment and distress. This is the case for contracts for the provision of a holiday trip, etc., where the contract is, in essence, selling enjoyment.

47 B

A contract does not come into existence unless there has been an offer and acceptance. The advertisement is an invitation to treat, not an offer. Petra has made an offer but it has not been accepted by John. John can therefore sell the car to Gabriel and Petra cannot sue John for breach of any contract.

48 £2,000 × 1.2 (TO ADD VAT) × 10.5% (BASE RATE + 8%) × 30 ÷ 365 = **£20.71**.

C Additional compensation of £70 can be claimed since the debt is between £1,000 and £10,000 (£40 can be charged on debts less than £1,000 and £100 on debts over £10,000).

49 A

50 A

51 B

An action for price is used to force payment of the debt

52

	Tick
The injured party may recover damages for any loss suffered.	✓
The injured party may force the other party to complete the contract.	✓
The injured party may bring an 'action for price'.	✓
The injured party may fine the other party.	

53 A

54 C

DATA PROTECTION ACT

55 A

56 A

57 D

58

	Tick
Have access to a copy of the data held.	✓
Ask to know why the data is being processed.	✓
Seek compensation through the courts for damage or distress caused by the loss, destruction, inaccuracy or unauthorised disclosure of their data.	✓
Apply to the courts or Registrar for inaccurate data to be corrected or removed from their files.	✓

OTHER LEGISLATION

59 A

The Unfair Contract Terms Act 1977 declares such exclusions to be void.

60

	True	**False**
The Consumer Rights Act allows a buyer to return faulty goods within 30 days and receive a full refund	✓	
Under the Consumer Rights Act, a fault is presumed to have existed at purchase if the faulty goods are returned within three month of purchase		✓
The Consumer Credit Act gives additional protection on purchases of between £100 and £30,000 made with a debit or credit card		✓
The Trade Descriptions Act applies to both goods and services	✓	

Under the Consumer Rights Act, a fault is presumed to have existed at purchase if the faulty goods are returned within six month of purchase. The Consumer Credit Act only gives additional protection if a credit card (not a debit card) is used.

61 C

62 B

63 D

GRANTING CREDIT

GRANTING CREDIT PROCEDURES

64 NOTE – ONLY 3 EXTERNAL SOURCES REQUIRED

Trade credit references/supplier references

Creditworthiness can be checked by asking the customer to supply trade references from other suppliers (usually two). It can be assumed that customers will not quote suppliers likely to give a bad report therefore it is unwise to rely on this procedure alone. Used in conjunction with other information, this procedure however may be helpful.

Bank references

Requests to the bank need to detail:

- the amount of credit you envisage giving the customer
- the credit period.

Bank replies are usually structured in one of three ways:

- an unqualified, positive assurance
- a general indication that the firm is operating normally
- a guarded statement, indicating that 'capital is fully employed' or 'we are unable to speak for your figures'.

Credit reference agency reports

The credit rating provided by the agency indicates the average amount of credit given to the firm. This helps the credit manager to assess the relative size of the proposed credit limit to the potential customer.

The problems with agency reports are as follows:

- New companies have no track record. It is therefore very difficult to form a judgement.
- It takes time for current information to be analysed and fed into computer/appraisal systems. It is possible for very relevant information (such as the collapse of a major customer) not to be in a report.

Management accounts

If available management accounts can be useful for identifying future plans (such as production and sales levels) of a company.

Credit circle meetings

A credit circle is a group of people with a common interest, for example a trade association. These people meet on a regular basis to share information on credit related matters, such as late payers.

Official publications

The press provide an up-to-date commentary on the situation within local and national companies. If the proposed customer is a big national company, reading The Financial Times enables the credit manager to keep up-to-date with half-yearly reports, comments on the customer as well as keeping abreast of industry trends and problems. Smaller more local companies are commented upon in regional and local papers.

Trade journals are often produced weekly or monthly. Trade journals are another valuable source of information and commentary on trends and results.

The sales director should have little input when assessing whether to grant credit. She has knowledge of the industry but not necessarily knowledge of credit management and maintaining liquidity. She is rewarded for new customers so her objectivity could be compromised.

65

(a) Only 2 required

Sales representatives on client visits can be asked to

1 Remind customers whenever an account is overdue. This ensures the person responsible for orders is aware the account has not been paid within the terms. He/she/they is likely to be able to influence the Accounts Payable department from within the business.

2 Observe the premises to gain an impression of whether the business looks busy/well managed By witnessing how active the business is, the representative is in a position to say whether business is quiet. This might indicate that less cash will be available to settle accounts with suppliers.

3 Take note of any internal notice boards or overheard comments that might indicate the business is having difficulties Notices asking for volunteers to work overtime would indicate that business is booming and that cash is available to pay suppliers. Rumours of redundancies might be a clue to be vigilant if the account becomes overdue.

(b) Only 3 required

1 Follow a set procedure when invoices have not been settled within the credit terms. A telephone call or a letter notifying a client that the date due has passed and the account may be put on stop is likely to lead to payment more quickly than ignoring it. The procedure will give the clerk a date on which an overdue account should be passed to a debt collection agency or when to initiate court action. This is easier than leaving the decision of when to initiate action to the clerk.

2 Notifying the Finance Manager of any reasons offered by customers for non-payment. Any claims that goods supplied were not satisfactory can be addressed quickly so that no reason remains for late or non-payment of an invoice.

3 Notifying the sales representatives. This can enable the sales representatives to make personal contact with the firm and remind them of their obligation to pay on time.

4 Keeping records of credit checks carried out on new credit customers. These can be used to compare with the actual payment records from the customers, and enable prompt responses to any not keeping to terms.

66 B

67

	Internal	**External**
Trade references.		✓
Sales representatives' knowledge.	✓	
Credit Agency.		✓
Bank references.		✓
Supplier references.		✓
Ratio calculations.	✓	

68 B

69 C

70 D

Trade will be possible, but only on a cash basis.

71 A

72 B

Pareto's principle is another name for the 80/20 rule.

73

	Tick
Financial accounts	✓
Aged receivable analysis	
Copies of outstanding invoices	
Draft contract for trade	
Trade references	✓
Bank references	✓

74

Company LTD
A Building
Business Park
County
CT3 9AP

Finance Director
Customer Ltd
Industrial Park
Town

Today 2011

Dear Sir

Re: Request for credit facilities

Thank you for your enquiry regarding the provision of credit facilities by us. As you are a new customer and unable to provide trade references or a set of financial statements we are unable to be able to offer credit facilities at this time.

We would of course be delighted to trade with you on a cash basis. If you do not wish to trade on this basis and would like to enquire about credit terms in the future then we would be delighted to examine your current year's financial statements when they are available.

Thank you for your interest in our company.

Yours faithfully

A Person

A Person
Credit Manager

PERFORMANCE INDICATORS

75 C

76 B

Payable days give the credit controller how long on average the company takes to pay its debts. The other ratios are important, but payable days are likely to be of the most interest.

77 A

78 A

79 A

(150 + 300 + 25)/(230 + 90) = 1.48

80 B

(300 + 25)/(230 + 90) = 1.02

81 A

(300/2,700) × 365 = 40.55 days

82 B

(230/1,300) × 365 = 64.58 days

83 D

(150/1,300) × 365 = 42.12 days

84 C

(550/2,700) × 100 = 20.3%

85 C

550/75 = 7.33 times

86 B

16,000/(16,000 + 38,512) × 100 = 29.4%.

Remember in CRDM to only include non-current liabilities in debt.

87 43.0%

= PBIT/Revenue × 100 = 27,657/64,323 × 100 = 43.0%

88 C

(12,506 + 5,006)/(15,000+3,000) = 0.97

89 D

27,657/(38,512 + 16,000) × 100 = 50.7%

90 C

12,506/64,323 × 365 = 70.97 days

91 A

(1,250/2,250) × 100 = 55.6%

92 B

(825/2,250) × 100 = 36.7%

93 D

490/275 = 1.8

94 D

(240/2,250) × 365 = 39 days

95 A

(275/1,000) × 365 = 100 days

96 B

(150/1,000) × 365 = 55 days

97 B

(60,000/300,000) × 365 days = 73 days

98 21.57 DAYS

£2,600 ÷ (5,500 × £8) × 365

CREDIT LIMIT ASSESSMENT (RATING SYSTEM)

99 (a)

Trot Limited	**Indicator**	**Rating**	**Indicator**	**Rating**
Year	**20X2**		**20X1**	
Operating profit margin	–2,100/9,000 × 100 = –23.33%	–5	–900/11000 × 100 = –8.18%	–5
Interest cover	0	–30	0	–30
Current ratio	3,900/4,200 = 0.93	–20	4,000/3,600 = 1.11	–10
Gearing	2,000/(2,000 + 2,100) × 100 = 48.78%	10	1,000/(1,000 + 4,400) × 100 = 18.52%	20
		–45		–25

(b) C Reject

100 (a)

Walk Limited	**Indicator**	**Rating**	**Indicator**	**Rating**
Year	**20X2**		**20X1**	
Operating profit margin	3,250/22,500 × 100 = 14.44%	10	1,375/20,000 × 100 = 6.88%	5
Interest cover	3,250/625 = 5.2 times	10	1,375/625 = 2.2	0
Current ratio	5,750/3,750 = 1.53	10	5,000/3,250 = 1.54	10
Gearing	6,250/(6,250 + 7,000) × 100 = 47.17%	10	6,250/(6,250 + 5,250) × 100 = 54.35%	0
		40		15

(b) A Accept

101 (a)

Canter Limited	**Indicator**	**Rating**	**Indicator**	**Rating**
Year	**20X1**		**20X0**	
Operating profit margin	675/9750 × 100 = 6.92%	5	1,125/9,000 × 100 = 12.5%	10
Interest cover	675/750 = 0.9 times	–20	1,125/375 = 3 times	0
Current ratio	3,900/3,150 = 1.24	–10	2,475/2,100 = 1.18	–10
Gearing	7,500/(7,500 + 3,825) × 100 = 66.23%	–20	3,000/(3,000 + 3,900) × 100 = 43.48%	10
		–45		10

(b) The above table show Canter Limited's credit rating has reduced substantially and is now rated as a high risk. However, there are certain factors which are in its favour. These include the following:

- A good trading history over several years, although recently they have made some late payments.
- The expansion plan and the fact that the bank has given loans for the purchase of new assets is a good sign.
- New customers have ordered goods and have indicated that they will continue in 20X2.
- The company is still liquid with cash at bank at the year end.

It is worth considering taking some kind of security over the business or personal guarantees from the directors or to consider retention of title clauses.

Note: There is no right decision and as long as the credit controller considers all the issues and makes a reasoned decision credit will be awarded.

102

(a)

B Limited	**Indicator**	**Rating**	**Indicator**	**Rating**
Year	**20X1**		**20X0**	
Operating profit margin	1,450/9,000 × 100 = 16.1%	20	1,350/7,000 × 100 = 19.3%	20
Interest cover	1,450/250 = 5.8	10	1,350/250 = 5.4	10
Quick ratio	(2,280 – 600)/600 = 2.8	10	(1,800 – 500)/500 = 2.6	10
Gearing	3,000/(3,000 + 3,680) × 100 = 45%	–20	3,000/(3,000 + 2,800) = 52%	–40
		20		0

(b) A Accept

103

(a)

Oville Limited	**Indicator**	**Rating**	**Indicator**	**Rating**
Year	**20X1**		**20X0**	
Operating profit margin %	400/8,000 × 100 = 5.00	30	150/5,200 × 100 = 2.88	0
Interest cover	400/150 = 2.67	0	150/50 = 3.00	60
Acid test	(3,150 – 1,400)/2,750 = 0.64	–30	(2,030 – 630)/1,500 = 0.93	–30
Gearing %	1,750/(1,750 + 2,500) × 100 = 41.2%	–60	875/(875 + 2,280) × 100 = 27.7%	30
		–60		60

(b) A Accept

104

(a)

Foreman Limited	**Indicator**	**Rating**	**Indicator**	**Rating**
Year	**20X1**		**20X0**	
Operating profit margin %	2,000/12,000 × 100 = 16.67	10	2,000/10,000 × 100 = 20.00	20
Trade payables days	1,000/5,500 × 365 = 66.36	–10	700/4,000 × 365 = 63.88	–10
EBITDA/Total debt	(2,000 + 800)/5,000 = 0.56	10	(2,000 + 500)/3,000 = 0.83	20
Interest cover	2,000/1,500 = 1.33	–10	2,000/1,000 = 2	0
Total score		0		30

(b)

Clay Limited	**Indicator**	**Rating**	**Indicator**	**Rating**
Year	**20X1**		**20X0**	
Operating profit margin %	2,700/7,000 × 100 = 38.57	20	2,250/6,000 × 100 = 37.50	20
Trade payables days	700/2,500 × 365 = 102.20	–20	600/2,000 × 365 = 109.50	–20
EBITDA/Total debt	(2,700 + 300)/4,500 = 0.67	20	(2,250 + 350)/4,500 = 0.58	10
Interest cover	2,700/1,700 = 1.59	–10	2,250/1,500 = 1.50	–10
Total score		10		0

(c) **Foreman Limited**

Foreman was rated as very low risk in 20X0 explaining why credit was given.

Foreman is requesting a large increase in credit; however, after review of the 20X1 ratios the credit score has indicated that Foreman has become a medium risk.

Although Foreman has generated more revenue, margins have slipped, but the key reason for the change in credit rating is the extra debt that Foreman has taken on board.

Debt has increased from £3m to £5m with an increase in the cost of financing this debt.

Possible options:

- Extend the credit limit as requested.
- Extend the credit limit but not by as much as requested.
- Freeze the credit limit at the current level.
- Remove the credit facility.

Considerations:

- Growth in revenue and willingness of banks to lend finance indicates a relatively healthy company.
- It appears that Foreman has raised finance (£3m to £5m total debt movement) and invested that in Capital expenditure (depreciation charge increases year on year).
- It will take time for these new assets to generate increased revenue and profit.
- If we withdraw credit then we could lose an existing customer who may give us growing sales in the future.

Recommendation:

- The credit limit should be frozen until Foreman can convince us that the capital investment will generate increased profit.

Clay limited

Clay is rated as low risk indicating that the credit request should be accepted. However it should be noted that Clay was rated marginal between medium risk and low risk in 20X0.

Also trade payables are high which could indicate short term cash flow issues, but trade payables days have slightly reduced.

Recommendation:

- Accept application for credit.
- Monitor payment dates closely and ensure that Clay Limited complies with our credit terms.

105

1 **Current ratio** – this ratio shows the amount of current assets in relation to the current liabilities and is a measure of the liquidity of the business. If a company has a ratio of 2:1 it means that for every £1 of current liabilities the company has £2 of current assets. Therefore in theory the business is liquid.

2 **Receivables' collection period in days** – the average time taken to collect the cash from customers. This indicates the time scale over which the company receives cash from its credit customers. This is not directly relevant to the decision whether or not to grant credit but it can give useful information about how the company operates.

3 **Payables' payment period in days** – the average time taken to pay suppliers. This is directly relevant to the decision whether or not to grant credit as it indicates the general time scale over which the company pays its current credit suppliers. It is desirable for the receivables' collection period to be shorter than the payables' payment period. This way the company collects what is due before it has to pay out to its own payables. However, with a competitive market it is not always possible to arrange the cash flows so advantageously. Nevertheless, the ratios should not be too different to avoid a negative cash flow.

4 **Inventory holding period in days** – the average time taken to sell inventory. This ratio indicates whether a business's inventory is justified in relation to its sales. If inventory holding increases in terms of number of days, this may indicate excess stocks or sluggish sales.

5 **Operating profit margin** – how much of the revenue is operating profit i.e. how much of the revenue is left once expenses are paid. A low margin indicates low selling prices or high costs or both. Comparative analysis over a number of years will give an indication as to how well a company controls its costs and revenues – if the ratio increases more control is likely to be in place.

6 **Interest cover** – how many time the profit before interest will cover the interest payments due. This gives an indication of how easily the company can maintain payments of its loan and debenture interest and therefore gives additional information about the riskiness of the company. The purpose of the assessment of the customer's financial statements is to determine the likelihood that they will pay their trade debts on time. If a company has long-term loan capital in its capital structure, then the interest on this must be paid thereby reducing the profits available to make other payments such as those to trade payables. Therefore the interest cover is additional evidence of the risk associated with the company.

7 **Gearing** – the amount of long-term capital (owed to third parties) in the company's capital structure as this can be an element of the riskiness of a company. The greater the extent to which a company is financed by debt, the greater is the risk of investing in it.

106

	20X1	20X0
1 Operating profit margin	47,500/350,000 × 100 = 13.6%	15,500/230,000 × 100 = 6.7%
2 Interest cover	47,500/5,000 = 9.5 times	15,500/5,000 = 3.1 times
3 Current ratio	124,357/45,939 = 2.7	60,582/18,164 = 3.3
4 Receivable days	62,789/350,000 × 365 = 65.5 days	41,918/230,000 × 365 = 66.5 days
5 Payable days	23,980/227,500 × 365 = 38.5 days	18,164/149,500 × 365 = 44.3 days
6 Gearing ratio	15,000/(15,000 + 213,418) × 100 = 6.6%	50,000/(50,000 + 22,418) × 100 = 69.0%

A £10,000 credit limit for Wright Ltd should be granted given the ratios above. The operating profit and interest cover have improved from 20X0 to 20X1. Receivable days have remained constant over the 2 years available. Payable days are approximately 38.5 days which is an improvement from 20X0; this also appears to be an acceptable payment term. The company is currently geared on a small proportion of debt. The only ratio that has declined is the current ratio from 3.3 to 2.7 in 20X1.

107

	20X1	20X0
Gross profit %	422/1,050 × 100 = 40.19%	337/850 × 100 = 39.65%
Operating profit %	107/1,050 × 100 = 10.19%	82/850 × 100 = 9.65%
Return on capital employed	107/(650 + 100) × 100 = 14.27%	82/(410 + 100) × 100 = 16.08%
Current ratio	400/160 = 2.5:1	320/100 = 3.2:1
Quick or acid test ratio	160/160 = 1:1	120/100 = 1.2:1
Receivable days	160/1,050 × 365 = 55.6 days	120/850 × 365 = 51.53 days
Payable days	90/628 × 365 = 52.31 days	60/513 × 365 = 42.69 days

- The gross profit and operating profit percentages have remained largely static with a minor increase in both. This indicates that any increase in sales has been mainly matched by a corresponding increase in costs.
- The ROCE has declined – there is less return for the money or assets invested in the business, but there has been a big investment in non-current assets in 20X1.
- The current and quick ratios have got worse meaning that there are less assets to cover the liabilities. Looking at the statement of financial position it appears that Red Kite Ltd does not have any available cash of their own as they have a bank overdraft, which has increased by £20,000.
- The receivable and payable days have both increased from X0 to X1 – this could indicate that Red Kite Ltd is having problems with its credit control department. Ideally receivable days should be shorter than payable days as this means that Red Kite Ltd should have collected the cash from the receivables before needing to pay it to their payables.
- Red Kite Ltd's performance indicators give an indication that they might be starting to overtrade.

108 The company turnover has increased by 54% from £2.6 million to £4 million. This is a strong sign of overtrading.

- Correct calculation of the increase.
- The fact that turnover has increased is not necessarily a strong sign of overtrading as many indicators have to be considered to demonstrate overtrading – including reduced margins, increased current assets, trade cycle days and cash flow.

The operating profit has increase from £100,000 to £250,000. This means that more cash is available to pay debts.

- This does not mean that more cash is available to pay debts. It all depends on where the profit has gone for the period – has it been invested or tied up in inventory, receivables or non-current assets?
- To consider the liquidity of a company, changes in assets and liabilities have to be investigated.
- Profit has risen along with turnover which indicates that turnover has not been chased at the detriment of profit. There is a slight decline in the gross profit margin which may indicate some changes to production cost or some discounting of sales price.

The interest cover has increased from 2.0 to 2.5 times which means that the company is in a worse position than last year.

- This is not correct as an increase in interest cover means that there is more profit to cover finance costs or interest repayments and that loans, and therefore the interest payments have reduced.

The current ratio should be 2 which means that the company is insolvent.

- This is a common misunderstanding. It is not possible to state that there is a perfect ratio. All that can be said is that the higher the ratio is the better.
- The current ratio has declined and the company is now using its overdraft facility with cash tied up in inventory and receivables.

The trade receivables balance has increased by £300,000 which supports the conclusion of overtrading.

- The trade receivables balance has increased but the trade receivable collection period has reduced which shows that the company is coping with the increase in credit sales.

The trade payables are down from 146 days to 141 implying the company is struggling to get credit from its suppliers.

- The way this could be interpreted is that the company are taking less time to pay their debts which is a positive sign.
- The time period is very long – approximately 5 months – which would indicate problems with cash flow.

The inventory has increased by £440,000 which supports the conclusion of overtrading.

- Inventory levels will need to increase to support the increasing sales, which is where most of the cash has been invested.
- This along with the increase in inventory days would indicate that there has been too much investment in inventory.

Gearing has increased with means that the banks are not happy to lend money to the business.

- Gearing increasing would actually be an indication that the company is accessing more debt finance that equity finance i.e. the banks are happy to lend money.
- So long as there is cash to pay the increased finance cost then an increase in finance should not be a problem.

I agree with your conclusion is that credit should **not** be given. There are positive signs of increases in revenue, operating profit margin and a decrease in payable days but combined with the use of the use of the overdraft facility would indicate that there are cash flow problems currently.

109 Profitability

- Revenue has decreased by a small amount (3.5%)
- Gross profit has fallen by a similar amount to revenue (3.1%)
- Operating profit has fallen by 27%
- Interest cover has improved from 3.75 to 4.8.

Clare Ltd has moved from finance leases to operating leases which may have been more expensive to administer thus affecting operating profit. This change will also reduce finance costs having the positive impact on interest cover. The business is now more reliant on operating leases than finance leases.

Liquidity

- Current ratio is better in X1 than X0 (1.08 vs 0.70)
- Receivables period has decreased/improved slightly from 33.0 days to 31.0 days
- Payable and inventory periods have also decreased.

Clare Ltd does seem to be managing its debt collection and payment so it would appear that working capital is being managed. Liquidity appears to have improved.

Gearing and risk

- Gearing has decreased substantially
- The level of borrowing in absolute terms has also significantly reduced.

Clare Ltd has reduced the level of borrowing that is shown on the face of the financial statements but is now reliant on nearly £6 million non-cancellable short term leases which are shown as a note to the statements. If the leases had been included in gearing then it would be extremely high.

Conclusion

Ratios appear to be acceptable but the leases are a concern.

Defer a decision until further information is made available re:

- Future forecasts for the agricultural industries
- Future cash flow projections from Clare Ltd.

If credit is granted consider retention of title clauses, credit insurance and/or directors' guarantees.

110 **Nicville's statement of profit or loss looks healthy. There is an increase in revenue and an increase in profit from X0 to X1; but both the gross profit margin and the operating profit margin have declined slightly showing that Nicville may not have complete control over their costs.**

The interest cover has declined but there has not been an increase in the long term loan. More information is required to explain why the finance cost has increased from X0 to X1.

Nicville is highly geared, which is generally more risky. There is more debt finance than equity finance in both years but there has been a significant reduction in the gearing from X0 to X1 which has been caused by an increase in retained earnings.

Nicville has a good liquidity levels. They are not using an overdraft and the receivable, inventory and payable days have all remained reasonably static. Receivable days have increased/worsened slightly from 58 to 59 days, inventory days have increased slightly from 58 to 63 and payable days have decreased from 88 to 73 days. Nicville have a working capital cycle of 28 days (58 + 58 – 88) in X0 which means that what has been purchased is being sold and converted into cash in approximately 28 days. Nicville were collecting the cash from receivables quicker than they were paying the payables which is a good thing. The working capital cycle was 49 days (63 + 59 – 73) in X1. This would indicate that Nicville have lost a bit of control over the working capital in the business but this mainly because their payables days have reduced which is positive with regards granting credit.

Based on the above analysis I would offer Nicville credit terms but for a lower amount to start with as the business appears to be liquid. The account should be closely monitored and it may be worth adding a retention of title clause to the contract.

111 (a)

Grenouille Limited	**20X1 Indicator**	**20X0 Indicator**
Gross profit margin %	4,000/10,000 × 100 = 40.00	2,000/6,000 × 100 = 33.33
Operating profit margin %	1,800/10,000 × 100 = 18.00	1,300/6,000 × 100 = 21.67
Trade payable days	800/6,000 × 365 = 49	450/4,000 × 365 = 41
Inventory holding days	1,300/6,000 × 365 = 79	450/4,000 × 365 = 41
Current ratio	(1,300 + 1,300 + 700)/800 = 4.13	(450 + 750 + 300)/450 = 3.33

(b)

Email

To: Credit controller **Date:** Today

From: AAT Technician **Subject:** New Customer Grenouille Limited

Please find below my observations and recommendations for new customer Grenouille limited.

Profitability

The revenue has increased by **66.67%** which means that the company has **either sold more units or increased the price of its product**.

The gross profit margin has increased by **20.01%**.

The company may have **increased the sales price of the product and/or reduced the costs of production**.

The most important indicator for profitability is the **operating profit margin** which has reduced by **16.94%**.

This is not a concern as absolute profits have increased substantially.

Liquidity

The current ratio provides **a rough measure of the short term solvency of the organisation**.

In this case it has increased and is **greater than previous years which is a sign of improved solvency**.

The inventory holding period has **increased**. **This appears to be a strong sign of overtrading**.

The trade payables payment period in days has **increased** by **8** days.

It appears that the company is funding its expansion by increasing long term borrowings and retaining profit.

I recommend that **credit be granted**.

112 (a) Overtrading occurs when a company expands too rapidly and has insufficient working capital and insufficient cash available to support the increased level of trading.

Sales revenue

Sales revenue has increased by 80% from 20X2 to 20X3 which is probably due in part to the newly motivated sales team. Such a steep increase could indicate overtrading.

Trade receivables

Trade receivables have also increased in absolute terms by 200%. This is a much greater increase than the increase in sales revenue. This could be a sign of overtrading but could also be due to the company no longer having a credit controller.

It could also be a sign that the company is extending credit to customers with a higher risk profile in an attempt to increase sales.

Trade receivables collection period in days

Customers are now taking an average of 70 days to settle their debts compared to 42 days in 20X2. This is probably a direct result of the company losing its credit controller. The company has extended its credit period to 60 days for new customers, but on average debts are being collected 10 days later than this. The increase in trade receivables days is a warning sign that the company may be overtrading.

Trade payables

Trade payables have increased by 257% in 20X3 but this is probably due to the increase in cost of sales required to support the additional sales. Considered on its own, this is not a sign of overtrading.

Trade payables payment period in days

Trade payables days have almost doubled from 35 days to 64 days. An increase in trade payables days is a possible warning sign of overtrading when considered together with a rapid increase in sales and an increase in trade receivables days. 64 days is longer than our credit terms of 30 days.

Inventories

The level of inventories held at the end of 20X3 is 255% higher than at the end of 20X2. This supports the idea that inventory has been increased to satisfy the sales levels. This is a possible sign of overtrading if the inventory holding period has also increased.

Inventories holding period in days

Inventory days have increased from 36 days to 66 days. This is about the same increase as for trade payables which suggests that the company is financing its expansion using credit from suppliers. A company that is overtrading would usually have increased levels of inventory accompanied by longer inventory holding period. This increases the possibility of inventory obsolescence.

Gross profit

In absolute terms gross profit has increased by £270,000. This would not support or deny overtrading.

Gross profit margin

The gross profit margin has reduced from 30% to 24%. This could be due to a reduction in selling price to encourage an increase in sales volume. A decrease in margins is a warning sign of overtrading but may also be due to other factors.

Operating profit

The operating profit is higher in 20X3 than in 20X2 in absolute terms which is due to the feed through of absolute gross profit.

Operating profit margin

The operating margin has also reduced by 3%. This is a smaller reduction than the decrease in gross profit which suggests that expenses are being more tightly controlled in 20X3. A fall in margins is a warning sign of overtrading.

Interest cover

Interest cover has decreased which can be linked to the fall in absolute operating profit. Bank loans and overdrafts have more than doubled in the year which will lead to an increase in finance costs.

Current ratio

The current ratio has reduced from 2 to 1.68 from 20X2 to 20X3. Current liabilities are covered by current assets.

Quick ratio

Although there has been a decline in the quick ratio Rumpleteazer can still comfortably meet its current liabilities by its current assets without the need to convert inventories to cash. Neither the current ratio nor the quick ratio suggests that Rumpleteazer is overtrading.

Other points

The cash position of Rumpleteazer has weakened significantly with no cash in hand in 20X3. This suggests an increased use of a bank overdraft. There has been investment in non-current assets which may explain the increase in bank loans and the reduction in cash in hand however the increase in debt has not been matched by increased investment by the owners.

The sharp increase in sales and the deterioration in working capital position suggest that Rumpleteazer is overtrading and may not have sufficient cash to continue operating at the current level.

(b) Rumpleteazer have asked for a significant increase in credit limit. It would be unwise to grant the increase because:

- The company appears to be overtrading.
- The company has increased its borrowing levels and is funding its working capital requirements through extended credit from suppliers.
- Loss of the credit controller suggests that the company may have difficulties collecting debts from customers.
- The trade payables days are 64 days and our credit terms are 30 days – it is unlikely we would be paid to terms.

Additional information that could be obtained:

- Trade references could be requested from companies already offering higher credit facilities to Rumpleteazer.
- Ascertain whether credit insurance could be obtained over sales invoices to Rumpleteazer.
- Need to review the trading history of Rumpleteazer with Mungojerry Ltd to ascertain whether they usually pay to terms.
- Would probably want to obtain an external credit report since there is no guarantee that the figures provided by Rumpleteazer are genuine.

COLLECTION OF DEBTS

COLLECTION OF DEBTS

113

	Tick
Finance charges.	✓
Increase in irrecoverable debts.	✓
Increase in liquidity.	
Increase in the amount of administration.	✓

114

	Tick
Extra administration.	✓
Increase in irrecoverable debts.	✓
Increased use of financing.	✓
Improved short term liquidity.	

115 D

116 C

117 C

118 B

119 £84,240

(£75,000 × 30%) + (£90,000 × 70% × 98%) = £84,240

120 D

SETTLEMENT DISCOUNTS

121 A

122 D

A trade discount is a discount agreed at the time the sale is made, examples are bulk purchase discounts for sales orders above a certain size, and discounts to regular customers. A discount offered for early payment is called a settlement discount or a cash discount.

123 B

124 A

(5/(100 – 5)) × (365/(28 – 14)) × 100 = 137.22%%

125 C

(2.5/(100 – 2.5)) × (365/(60 – 30)) × 100 = 31.2%

126 A

The supplier gains 60 days' use of the amount due at a cost of 4% i.e.

(4/(100 – 4)) × (365/(90 – 30)) × 100 = 25%

127 A

(1 + 5/(100 – 5)) ^ (365/(120 – 30)) – 1 = 0.231 = 23.1%

128 B

£400 × 95.5% = £382

(1 + 4.5/(100 – 4.5)) ^ (365/(28 – 7)) – 1 = 1.226 = 122.6%

129 C

(1 + 1/99) ^ (365/(44 – 14)) – 1 = 13%

130 The Sales Manager has found that her sales staff do not understand the annual percentage cost of the early settlement discounts that the company offers to customers.

Complete the following sentences:

If a customer pays promptly to take advantage of a 3% early settlement discount, we will receive 97% of the invoice total. This means that the discount we are giving the customer is **3 ÷ 97 × 100 = 3.09%** of the amount they pay us (2 decimal places). This is what it costs us to receive the cash earlier than our normal credit terms. It is the effective rate of interest.

If the normal credit terms require customers to pay within 60 days of receiving an invoice, and the discount applies if the customer pays within 21 days, we are offering the discount in return for paying 39 days earlier than our normal terms. There are **365 ÷ 39 = 9.36** discount periods of 39 days in a 365 day year (2 decimal places).

The annual percentage cost is found by **multiplying** the effective rate of interest and the discount periods in a year. The annual percentage cost of offering 3% discount to customers paying within 21 days rather than 60 days is **3.09 × 9.36 = 29%** (to the nearest whole percent).

131 C

(March £30,000) + (April £30,000 × 97.5% × 70%) = £50,475

132 A

£250 × 94.5% = £236.25

(5.5/94.5) × (365/(40 – 14)) × 100 = 81.7%

FACTORING, DISCOUNTING AND INSURANCE

133 B

Annual fee = £1,500,000 × 10% = £150,000

134 A

Annual sales revenue = £1,095,000	
Factoring fee £1,095,000 × 2.5%	= £27,375
Annual interest (90% × £180,000) × 12%	= £19,440
Savings in credit control costs	(£20,000)
Net cost of factoring	£26,815

135 £750,000

£1,250,145 × 80% = £1,000,116 is greater than the maximum allowed.

136 B

137 B

138 A

139 A

140 A

141 C

142 B

143 A

144 B

MANAGING TRADE RECEIVABLES

DEBT COLLECTION PROCEDURES

145 C

The 80/20 rule is also sometimes called Pareto's principle.

146 D

147 C

148 A

An aged receivables analysis lists the amounts and time invoices are outstanding for, for named receivables. It is a device used in credit control and receivables are contacted and 'chased' for amounts outstanding longer than the agreed credit period.

149 D

150 C

151 D

152

	Tick
The goods need to be in the possession of the seller	
Every invoice must show a retention of title clause	
The goods must be easily identifiable	✓
Goods should be in their original form	✓

153 C

154 £4,825

£5,000 – (£5,000 × £0.035) = £4,825

155 Aged receivables analysis

	Jan	Feb	Mar	Apr	Total
Invoice 234	118				
Invoice 365			135		
Invoice 379			232		
Invoice 391			71		
Invoice 438				145	
Totals	118		438	145	701

156 Advice – Proper policy should be followed with regards this debt but it may be worth involving the MD in the chasing of this debt.

157 Weaknesses

- No qualified credit control staff.
- Decision of granting credit is not necessarily based on fact – should ask for trade references and financial statements as a minimum.
- Invoice is raised on 1st of the month rather than on the day the goods are sent.
- Aged analysis is produced monthly but there is no indication that is acted upon.
- More active credit control is required with faster chase ups on outstanding debts – 1 month overdue is the first contact it needs to be 2 weeks with a follow up phone call a week later. It is too long to leave debts for 6 months before another review is done and passed to debt collectors or starting legal proceedings.

A suggested policy:

1. An order for goods is received by email, fax or phone (all phone calls are recorded).
2. Goods are delivered and a goods received note is signed by the customer.
3. The goods received notes are kept in a file in the accounts office.
4. An invoice will be issued a few days after delivery on 30 day terms.
5. An aged analysis of trade receivables report is produced monthly which is reviewed and outstanding debts are chased.
6. A reminder telephone call is made when the debt is 7 days overdue.
7. When a debt is 14 days overdue a letter is sent.
8. When the account is 28 days overdue the account will be put on stop.
9. The debt will either be placed in the hands of a debt collection company or legal proceedings could be instigated if the customer does not respond to calls or letters.

LEGAL ACTION

158 D

159

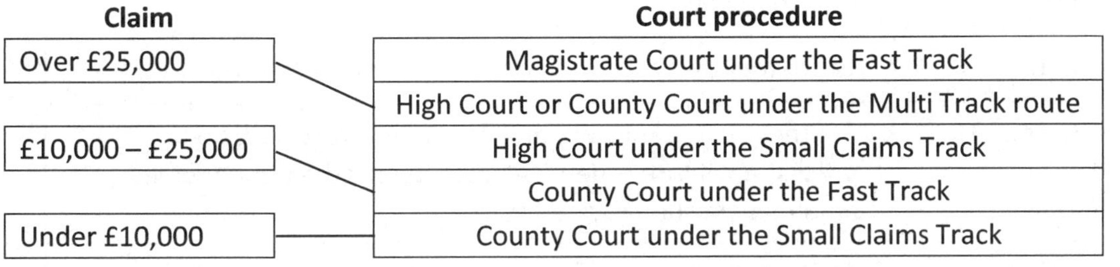

160 B

161 A

162 C

163 B

164 B

165

	Tick
Bankruptcy order	
Petition to the Court	✓
Appointment of Administrator	
Statutory demand	✓

166 C

167 D

168

	True	False
A CVA is applied where the business has no ongoing future		✓
A CVA is agreed between the business and creditors	✓	
A CVA is voluntary and hence not legally binding		✓
At least 75% of creditors must agree to the CVA	✓	
Under a CVA the business will pay back a proportion of the debts owed over a period of time	✓	
The CVA is monitored by the government		✓

CUSTOMER ANALYSIS

169

Customer	Action
Pink	No action needed.
Blue	Check the sales order and delivery note for any error.
Green	Put the account on stop until payment is received, do not process any more orders. A provision for the outstanding amounts may be provided for.
White	A chasing letter should be sent and the account should be on stop. A telephone call maybe needed to discuss credit terms.
Brown	No action needed.
Cerise	Contact the insolvency practitioner to register a claim and a provision should be made in the accounts.

170

(a) B The account is not overdue so no action is required.

(b) C Sack Limited's offices should be visited to identify the goods and register a retention of title claim with the insolvency practitioner.

(c) B Basket Limited should be contacted to confirm which invoices are being paid so the unallocated receipt can be allocated.

(d) A The unallocated cash needs to be adjusted by debiting the unallocated cash by £64,000 and crediting Barrow Limited accounts by £64,000.

(e) C CI claim will be made for £80,000; a provision needs to be made for £20,000 and VAT of £20,000 will be reclaimed from HMRC.

(f) B Send a copy of the delivery note which was signed by Satchel.

171

(a) B

(b) C

(c) C

(d) A

(e) B

172

(a) B Send a copy of the delivery note signed by the customer.

(b) D Contact the insolvency practitioner and register a claim with the credit insurer.

(c) Contact the credit insurer and claim £27,000 ÷ 120 × 100 × 70% = £15,750

Make a provision for (£27,000 ÷ 120 × 100) – £15,750 = £6,750

Claim VAT of £27,000 ÷ 120 × 20 = £4,500

(d) A Shelf should be contacted to confirm which invoices the payment relates to.

(e) A Debit the unallocated cash by £13,000 and credit the customer's account by £13,000.

(f) B The account is not overdue so no action is required.

173

Customer	**Action**	**Tick correct option**
Atkinson Limited	The account is overdue and a phone call should have been made on 18 April and a letter sent on 25 April.	✓
	The account is not overdue so no action is required.	
	The account should be on stop.	
Coppell Limited	Coppell Limited should be put on hold until the dispute is resolved.	
	Coppell Limited should be contacted to confirm which invoices are being paid so the unallocated receipt can be allocated.	✓
	The £13,000 should be returned to Coppell Limited.	
	The £13,000 should be allocated to the last invoice first.	
Beardsmore Trader	Arrange for redelivery of the order.	
	Request payment of debt in full.	
	Put the account on stop.	
	Request payment for the 19 correct items and if no payment is forthcoming contact the debt collection company.	✓

McGrath Limited	A provision should be made for the debt. Credit insurance is not valid.	✓
	A claim should be made with the insurance company.	
	Legal proceedings should be commenced.	
	The account should be put on stop.	
Olson Limited	Credit Insurance (CI) claim will be made for £25,000 and VAT of £5,000 will be reclaimed from HMRC.	
	CI claim will be made for £22,500; a provision needs to be made for £2,500 and VAT of £5,000 will be reclaimed from HMRC.	✓
	CI claim will be made for £24,000 and VAT of £6,000 will be reclaimed from HMRC.	
	CI claim will be made for £21,600; a provision needs to be made for £2,400 and VAT of £6,000 will be reclaimed from HMRC.	
	CI claim will be made for £27,000; a provision needs to be made for £3,000.	
Davenport Trader	Legal proceedings should be started. A provision should be made.	✓
	A telephone call should be made to chase the debt.	
	A letter should be sent.	
	The account should be put on stop.	

174

(a) D Contact the insolvency practitioner and register a claim with the credit insurer.

(b) C Contact John Limited, explain the terms and conditions of the discount. Ask for full payment of the outstanding amount.

(c) B Ask them to make an electronic (BACS) payment into our account.

(d) A Make a reminder phone call.

(e) B Ask the Managing Director to intervene and call his/her/their contact.

(f) D Start legal action with regards the older invoice.

175 Passage Ltd – Piaffe is going to need to make a provision for an irrecoverable debt or even write off the debt as there is very little chance of the cash being recovered, Passage have very few assets. Unsecured payables come far down the list when payments due to liquidation are made. A check should be made to see if the outstanding amount is on the statement of affairs of Passage. If Piaffe have a Retention of title clause then it may be possible to identify and return the assets purchased from Piaffe.

Vault Ltd – Vault should have received reminder letter and a telephone call and the account should be on stop as it is over 28 days overdue. The debt will not have been placed in the hands of a debt collector yet but this is the next course of action and a provision should be made. A further telephone call is required to chase payment as Vault Ltd is a regular customer.

Circle Ltd – Based on the value of these invoices it would appear that Circle Ltd is a major customer for Piaffe and therefore a meeting should be arranged to discuss their account. As there are rumours of overtrading it would be beneficial to request forecast accounts to be able to review their future liquidity. If no meeting is forthcoming then legal proceedings need to be started for the full outstanding amounts and a provision should be made for the full £144,000.

176 **Case Limited** – a new customer and has said that a cheque is in the post. Case should be asked for details of the cheque number and amount. It is not prudent to supply any further goods until the cheque has cleared. Depending on the source and credibility of the rumours it may be worth providing for this debt.

Holdall Limited – an overview of payment terms may be required as Holdall always eventually pays. A conversation with their finance director reminding him of the terms and conditions of credit may be required.

Cart Limited – the company should have waited for the cheque to clear and needs to ensure that this does not happen again. The debt needs to be placed in the hands of a debt collection agency and then legal proceedings need to be commenced when the debt is over 90 days overdue. A provision needs to be made.

Trolley Limited – Trolley Limited is in breach of contract as they did not notify Pocket of the poor quality goods until the second call. This needs to be explained to Trolley and if they do not agree to pay the matter needs to be placed in the hands of a solicitor as the debt collection company will not chase debts subject to dispute. Provision for non-collection should be made.

Trug Limited – Trug normal pay to terms so a conversation with their finance director reminding him of the terms and conditions of credit may be required. If this is unsuccessful then normal policy should be followed.

Tub Trader – the debt should be placed in the hands of the debt collectors. Often debt collectors are looked upon as a bit more of a threat and payment will happen. A provision should be made.

177 **Red** – A telephone call is needed to confirm which invoice the payment is against.

Yellow – Under the terms and conditions any fault should have been notified to Lamb Limited within 24 hours of receipt. The account should be placed on stop and Yellow should be notified that legal proceeding will be started if payment is not received. A provision for the debt should be made.

Violet – A telephone call is required to check postal details. A provision for the debt should be provided as there is uncertainty.

Amber – Lamb Limited needs to investigate how this could happen. The credit controller responsible for this needs to been spoken to. Telephone calls need to be made to locate Amber and chase for payment. Legal proceedings may be started if necessary. A provision should be provided at this stage, a write off may be necessary.

Mauve – Lamb Limited's MD should have a chat with Mauve's MD as usual credit control lines have not succeeded. Account may be put on stop until this conversation has been had.

Beige – Beige is already at its credit limit so no more orders should be processed until the payment is received.

Taupe – The account should be put on stop and credit terms revised.

Auburn – The insurance company should be contacted to reclaim the debt.

178 (a) (i)

- Workstation Ltd should review the order from Wardrobe to determine which product was ordered.
- If the order was for the correct grade then Wardrobe will need to pay for the goods to be returned and pay the administration charge of 5% if they do not want the goods.
- If they wish to keep the goods then Workstation Ltd can enforce the contract for payment.
- If Workstation Ltd believes that the debt will not be paid even if the error was down to Wardrobe then it may be more beneficial for Workstation Ltd to collect the goods and resell them rather than try and collect the debt.
- If the error was made by Workstation Ltd then the goods should be collected and a credit note should be raised.
- In addition if the error is due to Workstation Ltd then they should waive the administration charge.
- Workstation may decide that as a goodwill gesture the administration charge will be waived, and also perhaps the collection fee.
- It may be that the customer profitability in the course of the year is many times the additional cost if Workstation waives the charges.

(ii)

- All products manufactured by Workstation Ltd have a batch number stamped on them and so they should be easily identifiable.
- Workstation should be assertive with the receiver and insist that they be allowed to visit the premises to attempt to identify goods supplied by Workstation.
- Receivers often attempt to avoid ROT claims by initially stating that the claim is not valid in the hope that the supplier will not pursue the claim any further.

- The threat of legal action can be used if the receiver is not cooperating with a possible identification visit.
- The credit insurance company often have a specialist insolvency section who themselves are often ex insolvency practitioners/specialists.
- Workstation Ltd or the credit insurer should therefore visit Table Limited's premises immediately to identify any goods still on the premises so that an ROT claim can be made.
- The receiver should be present to confirm identification if possible.
- The credit insurer should be contacted and a claim made for £22,500, a provision for an irrecoverable debt of £7,500 should be made and VAT of £6,000 will be reclaimable from HMRC.

(iii)
- A telephone call is needed to confirm the address of Bureau Limited.
- If there is no response then further investigation will be required.
- A provision should be made for the debt. Credit insurance is not valid.

(b) Balance at 31st March = £12,000 + £6,500 – £1,500 + (£1,500 × 5%) – £10,000 = £7,075

Balance at 30th April = £7,075 + (£10,500 × 1.2) – £15,000 = £4,675

179

Customer	**Action**
Whiteside Limited	The raw materials will probably be covered by a valid ROT clause whereas the materials converted will not. The Credit Insurer needs to be contacted and a strategy to deal with the receiver needs to be agreed. Rooney does not want the goods back as they have a low scrap value and it will probably be better to negotiate with the receiver. The CI may still pay a claim for the losses incurred excluding VAT, a claim for irrecoverable debt relief at HMRC needs to be made and a provision for any additional losses may be needed.
Hughes Limited	If Rooney allows delivery before the cheque has cleared there is a risk that the cheque will not arrive and Hughes Limited may be attempting to defraud Rooney. Even though Hughes Limited will be within its credit limit Hughes Limited will not be adhering to agreed contractual terms. Hughes Limited needs to be contacted and told in polite terms that the goods cannot be released until the cheque has cleared. Also it can be pointed out that payment is 7 days overdue and as Hughes Limited is a new customer they have no trading history. Another credit controller may decide to ask for the cheque number and the date posted and then allow the credit limit to be exceeded for a few days. The ROT clause and risk of not being able to enforce the clause and resell also has to be considered.
Martin Limited	Balance 31st May = £5,800 + (£5,000 × 1.2) – (1,500 × £3 × 1.2) + (1,500 × £3 × 0.1 × 1.2) – £3,200 = £3,740 Balance 30th June = £3,740 + (£7,500 × 1.2) – £8,400 = £4,340

Bailey Limited	Rooney needs to consider negotiating with the receiver because the scrap value is only £2.50 per kilogram. Rooney needs to establish its minimum price to supply further goods. The further supplies are guaranteed to be paid as receiver expenses. The fact that there are surplus supplies of inventory will encourage Rooney to do a deal. A credit note may then need to be issued for the goods being transferred to the receivership and a provision may be needed for any amounts owing in excess of these goods.
Gidman Limited	Need to review the order to establish if Gidman ordered Z23, or X23. If Rooney made the mistake then Gidman can insist on redelivery of the correct goods. Rooney may decide to credit note the original invoice for £16,800 and reissue an invoice at a price of £21,600. Alternatively Rooney may decide to only charge the £14 per kilogram for Z23 as compensation. If on the other hand the error belonged to Gidman, then Rooney does not have to legally collect and redeliver but Rooney may decide to redeliver to provide excellent customer service and goodwill.

180 **Wham Limited** – there is dispute over the invoice amount as Wham state that a discount was promised by a salesman. Action needs to be taken to resolve this dispute which will probably mean speaking to the sales department to confirm the agreed price. Depending on the outcome of this either a credit note for the discount element should be issued or a request for full payment of the invoice made and normal procedures followed.

Spandau Trader – we should explain to Spandau it was them who ordered goods from us (not their client), if no payment is forthcoming following that conversation then refer the amount to debt collection/start legal proceedings.

FYC Limited – there is a dispute over the goods delivered. Action needs to be taken to resolve this dispute and the original item needs to be despatched (with the return of the better item). Then normal procedures followed.

Sting Limited – review the client file to ensure correspondence is in line with company policy. Assuming correspondence has been in line with company policy, start legal proceedings for the debt/refer the amount to debt collection.

Blue Trader – the account should be put on stop and legal proceedings should be started as there is no dispute. A provision should be made.

Hardcastle Trader – disclose that you have been trading historically with Hardcastle to the relevant authorities. Continue to follow normal procedures; however it would be prudent to provide for the amount as any money received could be as a result of money laundering.

Section 3

MOCK ASSESSMENT QUESTIONS

TASK 1 **(15 MARKS)**

(a) Which of the following is an example of consideration in a contract (tick all that apply)? **(1 mark)**

	Tick
Accepting an offer	
Being old enough to enter into legal relations	
Making an offer	
Paying for the goods	

(b) What is a requirement under the Consumer Rights Act? **(1 mark)**

A A contract details time and conditions of delivery

B Customers must be given a sample of goods sold

C Goods supplied must be of satisfactory quality

D Suppliers retain title to goods after sale

(c) Identify whether the following statements about the why the Data Protection Act exists are true or false. **(4 marks)**

The Data Protection Act exists:	True	False
To prevent businesses holding personal information without legitimate reason		
To ensure that information is maintained on employees		
To preserve records in business for a period of time		
To specify the records to be maintained in respect of information technology		

(d) A contract entered into as a result of a misrepresentation is: **(1 mark)**

A Enforceable

B Voidable

C Void

D Absolutely valid

(e) **What word fills the blank?** **(1 mark)**

Advertisements and shop windows displays are usually regarded as an .... rather than an offer.

A Consideration

B Acceptance

C Invitation to treat

D Invoice

(f) Sofia offers to sell her car to Tareq for £600. Tareq is unsure but, as he is leaving the sports club, asks Sofia if he can tell her by 9am the next day. Sofia agrees. Later that night Tareq meets Rick, a reliable mutual friend, who tells him that Sofia has decided to keep the car. Tareq visits Sofia at 8.30am and accepts the offer.

Is there a contract? **(1 mark)**

A Yes, because the revocation has not been communicated

B No, because revocation can be communicated by a reliable third party

C Yes, because Sofia has agreed to keep the offer open

D No, because the promise to keep the offer open was gratuitous

(g) **Match the description to terminology:** **(2 marks)**

Express terms	Specifically stated in a contract and binding
Conditions	Terms that are fundamental to the contract

(h) A customer owes £6,000 excluding VAT and the debt is 70 days late. The current Bank of England base rate is 1%.

Calculate the interest charge under the Late Payments of Commercial Debts Act to the nearest penny. **(1 mark)**

£

How much can be claimed by the company as a fixed sum compensation amount to help cover the costs of collecting the overdue debt? **(1 mark)**

£

(i) **Identify whether the following statements true or false.** **(2 marks)**

	True	False
Under the Consumer Rights Act, the remedies that exist for a customer are 'Refund, Repair, Replace'		
The Consumer Credit Act protects individuals who buy goods or services on their credit card for more than £250		

TASK 2 **(24 MARKS)**

You work as a credit control manager for Hardy Limited which uses a credit rating system to assess the credit status of new and existing customers.

The credit rating (scoring) system table below is used to assess the risk of default by calculating key indicators (ratios), comparing them to the table and calculating an aggregate score.

Credit rating (scoring) system	**Score**	**Credit rating (scoring) system**	**Score**
Operating profit margin		**Current ratio**	
Losses	–5	Less than 1	–20
Less than 5%	0	Between 1 and 1.25	–10
5% and above but less than 10%	5	Between 1.25 and 1.5	0
10% and above but less than 20%	10	Above 1.5	10
More than 20%	20	**Gearing**	
Payable days		Less than 25%	20
More than 91 days	–20	25% and above but less than 50%	10
61 to 90 days	0	More than 50% less than 65%	0
31 to 60 days	10	Between 65% and 75%	–20
Less than 30 days	20	Between 75% and 80%	–40
		Above 80%	–100

Risk	**Aggregate score**
Very low risk	Between 70 and 31
Low risk	Between 30 and 1
Medium risk	Between 0 and –24
High risk	Between –25 and –50
Very high risk	Above –50

The sales department has asked for a credit limit of £5,000 to be given to Smith Limited who is a potential new customer. The financial information below has been supplied by Smith Limited.

Accounts for Smith Limited Statement of profit or loss			**Statement of financial position**		
	20X0	**20X1**		**20X0**	**20X1**
	£	£		£	£
Revenue	**37,589**	**30,209**	**Non-current assets**		
Cost of sales	28,380	22,808	Property, plant and equipment	8,687	5,669
Gross profit	**9,209**	**7,401**	**Current assets**		
Distribution costs	3,755	3,098	Inventory	8,486	6,519
Administration costs	2,291	2,030	Trade receivables	8,836	6,261
Profit from operations	**3,163**	**2,273**	Cash	479	250
Finance cost	442	471			
Profit before taxation	**2,721**	**1,802**	**Total Assets**	**26,488**	**18,699**
Tax	1,038	650			
Profit for the year	**1,683**	**1,152**	**Equity**		
			Share capital	12,787	8,049
			Retained earnings	1,683	1,152
			Non-current liabilities		
			Long term loans	2,840	2,853
			Current liabilities		
			Trade payables	9,178	6,645
			Total equity and liabilities	**26,488**	**18,699**

(a) Complete the table below by calculating the key indicators (to 2 decimal places) for 20X0 and 20X1 for Smith Limited and rate the company using the credit rating scoring system. (18 marks)

Smith Limited	**Indicator**	**Rating**	**Indicator**	**Rating**
Year	**20X0**		**20X1**	
Operating profit margin				
Payable days				
Current ratio				
Gearing				
Total credit rating				

(b) Based on the result of your credit rating and the table below, comment whether the requested credit limit should be given to Smith Limited. (1 mark)

Rating	**Decision**
Very low or low risk current year and very low or low risk previous year	Accept
Very low or low risk current year and medium risk previous year	Accept
Very low or low risk current year and high or very high risk previous year	Request latest management accounts and defer decision
Very high risk or high risk current year	Reject
Medium risk current year and medium, low or very low risk previous year	Accept
Medium risk current year and high or very high risk previous year	Accept

A Accept

B Request latest management accounts and defer decision

C Reject

The sales department Silver Ltd has asked for a credit limit of £9,000 to be given to Gold Limited who is a potential new customer. The financial information below has been supplied by Gold Limited. Silver trades on 30 day terms.

Statement of profit or loss	**20X0** £	**20X1** £	**Statement of financial position**	**20X0** £	**20X1** £
Revenue	**135,000**	**191,000**	**Non-current assets**		
Cost of sales	80,000	120,000	Property, plant and equipment	60,000	82,000
Gross profit	**55,000**	**71,000**	**Current assets**		
Distribution costs	20,000	28,000	Inventory	10,000	27,424
Administration costs	9,688	8,620	Trade receivables	16,875	46,750
Operating Profit	**25,312**	**34,380**	Cash	4,852	2,000
Finance costs	2,250	7,500	**Total assets**	**91,727**	**158,174**
Profit before taxation	**23,062**	**26,880**	Equity		
Tax	8,764	10,214	Share capital	14,929	14,929
Profit for the year	**14,298**	**16,666**	Retained earnings	14,298	16,795
			Non-current liabilities		
			Loans	40,000	40,000
			Current liabilities		
			Overdraft	10,000	54,000
			Trade payables	12,500	32,450
			Total equity and liabilities	**91,727**	**158,174**

(c) Complete the email to the chief credit controller calculating and commenting on some key ratios. All calculations should be given to 2 decimal places. (5 marks)

* delete the wrong answers.

Email

To:	Credit controller	**Date:**	Today
From:	AAT Technician	**Subject:**	New Customer Gold Limited

Please find below my observations and recommendations for new customer Jones limited.

Profitability

The revenue has increased by [   ]%. Gross profit margin in 20X0 was 40.74 % and 37.17% in 20X1.

Operating profit itself has increased by 35.82% however the operating profit margin in 20X1 was 18.00% as compared to 18.75% in 20X0. This is a small drop compared to the gross margin.

This means that expenses have been well controlled/the cost of sales has been well controlled/sales have been well controlled*

Liquidity

Both the current ratio and the quick (acid test) ratio have deteriorated/improved*.

In order to understand the liquidity position further it is important to review the trade cycles and the individual components making up the ratios.

Inventory has increased by 174.24%. When compared to the increase in revenue this might indicate that Jones is planning further increases in sales.

The inventory holding period has increased from 45.63 days in 20X0 to [   ] days in 20X1. This means that funds are tied up in inventory.

The trade receivables collection period has improved/worsened*. Trade receivables have increased by 177.04%.

This might mean that Jones has an effective credit control team/Jones is offering more attractive terms to improve sales*

TASK 3 **(25 MARKS)**

Laurel Limited has been trading with Hardy Limited for several years and has, until recently, always paid to terms. Laurel has contacted Hardy Limited to request an increase in their credit limit from £50,000 to £100,000. Laurel Limited has supplied the accounts below.

Statement of profit or loss	**20X0**	**20X1**
	£000	£000
Revenue	**5,380**	**6,680**
Cost of sales	3,720	4,940
Gross profit	**1,660**	**1,740**
Distribution costs	490	610
Administration costs	220	270
Profit from operations	**950**	**860**
Finance cost	80	80
Profit before taxation	**870**	**780**
Tax	300	270
Profit for the year	**570**	**510**

Statement of financial position	**20X0**	**20X1**
	£000	£000
Non-current assets		
Property, plant and equipment	3,770	3,880
Current assets		
Inventory	550	600
Trade receivables	880	1,190
Cash	40	50
Total assets	**5,240**	**5,720**
Equity		
Share capital	2,710	3,120
Retained earnings	570	510
Non-current liabilities		
Loans	1,000	1,000
Current liabilities		
Trade payables	960	1,090
Total equity and liabilities	**5,240**	**5,720**

Laurel Limited	**20X0**	**20X1**
Operating profit margin %	17.7	12.9
Current ratio	1.5	1.7
Trade payable days	94 days	80 days
Gearing	23.4%	21.6%

The sales manager has reviewed the latest information provided by Laurel Limited and has made the following comments:

1 The company turnover has increased by 19% from £5.38 million to £6.68 million. This is a strong sign of overtrading.

2 The operating profit has decreased from £950,000 to £860,000. This means that less cash is available to pay debts.

3 The current ratio should be 2 which means that the company is insolvent.

4 The trade receivables balance has increased by £310,000 which supports the conclusion of overtrading.

5 The trade payables are down from 94 days to 80 days implying the company is struggling to get credit from its suppliers.

6 The inventory has increased by £50,000 which supports the conclusion of overtrading.

7 Gearing has decreased which means that the banks are not happy to lend money to the business.

8 My conclusion is that credit should not be given.

(a) Write a brief note dealing with each comment that the sales manager has made. Explain your reasoning and conclude as to whether credit should be given. (18 marks)

(b) Write notes to brief a new member of the credit control team explaining three sources of external information you could use (other than financial statements) when assessing whether to grant credit to a new customer. Comment on any ethical considerations you may need to be aware of. (7 marks)

TASK 4 **(12 MARKS)**

(a) A company's terms of payment are 28 days. It is offering a discount of 2% for payment within 14 days.

Calculate the following to two decimal places **(3 marks)**

The simple annual cost of the discount [ ] %

The compound annual cost of the discount [ ] %

(b) Cat has received a letter from the liquidator of Mouse Ltd. The liquidator has indicated that all unsecured creditors of Mouse will receive a dividend of 7p in the pound (£) later in the year. Cat is owed £10,000 by Mouse.

Calculate the amount that Cat should write off as an irrecoverable debt (ignore VAT). State your answer to the nearest penny **(1 mark)**

£

(c) If a business sells VAT taxable goods or services to a customer, the VAT element is paid to HMRC. If the customer does not pay for the goods or services irrecoverable debt relief can be claimed.

For a business to be able to claim back the VAT on an unpaid debt: **(3 marks)**

	True	**False**
The debt must be less than six month old		
The debt must be written off		
The VAT should have been paid to HMRC		

(d) **Which one of the following is an important aspect of liquidity management?** **(1 mark)**

	Tick
Liquidity management is important so that the company can ensure that cash is available to discharge commitments.	
Liquidity management is important so that the company can estimate how much cash is tied up in inventory and non-current assets.	
Liquidity management is important to ensure that a company does not make a loss.	
Liquidity management is important so that the shareholders can see how much return they will get on their investment.	

(e) Jump Ltd receives payments from customers 30 days after the month end. A 2.5% prompt payment discount will be offered from month 3 to customers who pay in the same month. It is expected that 70% of customers will take advantage of the discount. Expected sales revenue per month is as follows:

Month	Sales Revenue
2	£50,000
3	£65,000
4	£90,000

Expected cash receipts in month 4 will be: **(1 mark)**

£

Mariam has an irrecoverable debt of £10,800 including VAT at 20%. Mariam has credit insurance which covers 85% of the debt.

(f) **How much can Mariam claim under the insurance policy?** **(1 mark)**

£

(g) A company is looking to improve its cash flow and has been considering various finance products. The company has a balance on its sales ledger of £750,500 as at 31 August 20X3.

A finance company has offered to provide a facility where the company can borrow up to £600,000 or a maximum of 80% of the total outstanding sales ledger balance. The finance company administers the sales ledger on behalf of the company for a fee of £750 per month. The finance company will provide protection against irrecoverable debts.

ABC is offering **(1 mark)**

A without recourse factoring facility

B with recourse factoring facility

C credit insurance

D invoice discounting facility

The maximum amount available to borrow at the 31 August 20X3 is: **(1 mark)**

£

TASK 5 (12 MARKS)

(a) Company Alpha has a customer, Beta limited, who refuses to pay an outstanding amount of £12,000.

Which of the following will most likely deal with any action taken by Alpha to enforce the repayment of the debt? (1 mark)

A The High Court

B Multi Track route

C Small Claims Track

D Fast Track route

(b) Retention of title will normally be valid if: (4 marks)

	True	False
The contract contains a retention of title clause and the goods have been delivered		
The goods can be identified and have not been converted		
The goods have been attached to an immoveable machine and are part of the machine		
The goods subject to the clause must be in the customers possession		

(c) Which of the following is the best remedy for a breach of a contract where the supplier has delivered goods and the purchaser has refused to pay? (1 mark)

A Action for price

B Damages

C Repudiation

D Specific performance

(d) NG plc is owed £4,000 by a customer who refuses to pay, despite NG having secured a County Court Judgement against them. NG has gone back to the Court and a court bailiff has been given authority to take goods from the customer's home or business.

What is this arrangement known as? (1 mark)

A A warrant of execution

B An attachment of earnings order

C A garnishee order

D A charging order

(e) In order to petition the court for a winding up order the company must be owed at least: (1 mark)

A £75

B £750

C £7,500

D £1,000

(f) Complete the following sentences with phrases below: **(3 marks)**

The regular review of the aged trade receivable analysis should highlight customers who

[ ]

The credit manager needs to be looking for customers who are building up a significant outstanding amount.

Analysis of trade receivables can be simplified using [ ]

If this principle is applied to the trade receivables of a company it could help the credit manager focus the credit control team. The credit manager could assume that

[ ]

Phrase options

80% of the debts owed in value were due to only 20% of the customer accounts
60% of the debts owed in value were due to only 40% of the customer accounts
have recent debts cleared but have older outstanding amounts
are a bad credit risk
Pareto's Principle
Credit Circles

(g) Which TWO of the following are stages in a company winding up procedure? **(1 mark)**

	Tick
Bankruptcy order	
Petition to the Court	
Appointment of Administrator	
Statutory demand	

TASK 6 (12 MARKS)

Bowler Limited provides goods to the manufacturing sector. Each product is stamped with a batch number so that it can be identified. Standard terms and conditions are printed on the back of every invoice, which includes a retention of title clause that states that problems with goods must be notified to Bowler limited within 24 hours of delivery. Any goods that are returned are subject to an administration charge of 5%.

Today's date is 31 March 20X1.

The senior credit controller has asked you to put together notes on some customer accounts.

Credit control policy for Bowler Limited

Current credit control procedures once credit limit has been agreed:

1 An order for goods is received by email, fax or phone (all phone calls are recorded).

2 Goods are delivered and a goods received note is signed by the customer.

3 The goods received notes are kept in a file in the accounts office.

4 An invoice will be issued a few days after delivery on 30 day terms.

5 An aged analysis of trade receivables is produced monthly.

6 A reminder telephone call is made when the debt is 7 days overdue.

7 When a debt is 14 days overdue a letter is sent.

8 When the account is 28 days overdue the account will be put on stop.

9 The debt will either be placed in the hands of a debt collection company or legal proceedings could be instigated if the customer does not respond to calls or letters.

10 The business is credit insured, however insurance is only given for customers once they have a history of trade with the business of at least 12 months and have successfully paid for at least 3 invoiced amounts. Only 75% of the value of the debt is insured.

11 All sales invoices include VAT at the standard rate of 20% and VAT is reclaimed from HMRC.

(a) Review the information provided for each of the three customers below and prepare an action plan for collecting the amounts due. Your action plan should include a summary of the options available for the company to pursue and recommendations for provisions or write off of irrecoverable debts where appropriate. (10 marks)

Duckula

Duckula is a new customer and has said that the goods were not received in good condition. Duckula only raised a problem with the goods when they were called for the second time. They did not mention that the goods were poor quality on the first call or within 24 hours of delivery.

Clanger

Clanger has recently gone into liquidation. Clanger had been a customer for 5 years and has £48,000 outstanding.

(b) Greenbacks account has become corrupt on the system.

Balance at 1 April 20,000

Invoices raised:

5 April £7,500

12 May £12,500

Credit notes raised:

15 April £2,500 (subject to administration charge)

Bank receipts:

20 April £10,000

What is the balance on Greenbacks account at the end of April and the end of May?

(2 marks)

Section 4

ANSWERS TO MOCK ASSESSMENT QUESTIONS

TASK 1

(a)

	Tick
Accepting an offer	
Being old enough to enter into legal relations	
Making an offer	
Paying for the goods	✓

Consideration is something of value and money is the common form of consideration. Offer and acceptance are also necessary for a contract to take place. Parties to a contract must also have the capacity to contract. However, of the options given, only money is consideration.

(b) **C**

Consumer Rights Act legislation recognises the importance of goods being supplied of satisfactory quality to meet the needs of purchasers. Delivery is important in some instances, but is not necessary as part of a contract of sale. Often the buyer takes goods purchased away immediately. Samples may be used in buying and selling and the sample must be representative of the actual goods. However, the customer is not entitled to a sample. Retention of title is subject to the contract between buyer and seller. It usually ceases once the buyer has paid for the goods.

(c)

The Data Protection Act exists:	True	False
To prevent businesses holding personal information without legitimate reason	✓	
To ensure that information is maintained on employees		✓
To preserve records in business for a period of time		✓
To specify the records to be maintained in respect of information technology		✓

Data protection legislation is designed to protect the individual against information being kept for other than legitimate reasons. Certain information kept about employees for tax purposes, for example, is legitimately kept. Any information recorded about individuals is subject to data protection and other legislation.

(d) B

A contract entered into as a result of misrepresentation (fraudulent, negligent or innocent) is voidable.

(e) C

Advertisements and shop windows displays are usually regarded as an **invitation to treat** rather than an offer.

(f) B

The withdrawal of an offer can be made before acceptance and, if an offer is withdrawn, there cannot be offer and acceptance. A withdrawal of an offer can be communicated by a reliable third party and does not have to be made directly by the offeror to the offeree.

(g)

Express terms	→	Specifically stated in a contract and binding
Conditions	→	Terms that are fundamental to the contract

(h) INTEREST= £124.27

£6,000 × 1.20 (add VAT) × 9% (base rate + 8%) × 70 ÷ 365 = £124.27

COMPENSATION = £70

Since the amount owed is between £1,000 and £10,000 the fixed sum amount is £70.

(i)

	True	**False**
Under the Consumer Rights Act, the remedies that exist for a customer are 'Refund, Repair, Replace'	✓	
The Consumer Credit Act protects individuals who buy goods or services on their credit card for more than £250		✓

The Consumer Credit Act protects individuals who buy goods or services on their credit card for over £100 but not more than £30,000.

TASK 2

(a)

Smith Limited	Indicator	Rating	Indicator	Rating
Year	**2010**		**2011**	
Operating profit margin	(3,163/37,589) × 100 = 8.4%	5	(2,273/30,209) × 100 = 7.5%	5
Payable days	(9,178/28,380) × 365 = 118 days	–20	(6,645/22,808) × 365 = 106 days	–20
Current ratio	(8,486 + 8,836 + 479)/ 9,178 = 1.94	10	(6,519+6,261 + 250)/ 6,645 = 1.96	10
Gearing	(2,840/(2,840 + 14,470) × 100 = 16.4%	20	(2,853/(2,853 + 9,201)) × 100 = 23.7%	20
		15		15

(b) **ACCEPT**

(c)

Email

To: Credit controller **Date:** Today

From: AAT Technician **Subject:** New Customer Silver Limited

Please find below my observations and recommendations for new customer Jones limited.

Profitability

The revenue has increased by **41.48**%. Gross profit margin in 20X0 was 40.74% and 37.17% in 20X1.

Operating profit itself has increased by 35.82% however the operating profit margin in 20X1 was 18.00% as compared to 18.75% in 20X0. This is a small drop compared to the gross margin.

This means that **expenses have been well controlled**.

Liquidity

Both the current ratio and the quick (acid test) ratio have **deteriorated**.

In order to understand the liquidity position further it is important to review the trade cycles and the individual components making up the ratios.

Inventory has increased by 174.24%. When compared to the increase in revenue this might indicate that Jones is planning further increases in sales.

The inventory holding period has increased from 45.63 days in 20X0 to **83.41** days in 20X1. This means that funds are tied up in inventory.

The trade receivables collection period has **worsened**. Trade receivables have increased by 177.04%.

This might mean that **Jones is offering more attractive terms to improve sales**.

TASK 3

(a) **The company turnover has increased by 19% from £5.38 million to £6.68 million. This is a strong sign of overtrading.**

- The revenue has increased but by 24% not 19%.
- This is not necessarily a strong sign of overtrading as many indicators have to be considered to demonstrate overtrading – including reduced margins, increased current assets, trade cycle days and cash flow.

The operating profit has decreased from £950,000 to £860,000. This means that less cash is available to pay debts.

- This does not mean that less cash is available to pay debts. It all depends on where the profit has gone for the period – has it been invested or tied up in inventory, receivables or non-current assets?
- To consider the liquidity of a company, changes in assets and liabilities have to be investigated.
- Profit has fallen as revenue has increased which indicates that revenue has been chased at the detriment of profit. There is a decline in the gross profit margin which may indicate some changes to production cost.

The current ratio should be 2 which means that the company is insolvent.

- This is a common misunderstanding. It is not possible to state that there is a perfect ratio. All that can be said is that the higher the ratio is the better.
- The current ratio has increased and the company is not using its overdraft facility but most of the cash is tied up in receivables. This may indicate a credit control issue.

The trade receivables balance has increased by £310,000 which supports the conclusion of overtrading.

- The trade receivables balance has increased and the trade receivable collection period has increased which supports that the company may have credit control issues.

The trade payables are down from 94 days to 80 days implying the company is struggling to get credit from its suppliers.

- The way this could be interpreted is that the company are taking less time to pay their debts, which is a positive sign.

The inventory has increased by £50,000 which supports the conclusion of overtrading.

- Inventory levels need to increase to support increasing sales, but there has only been a 9% increase in inventory compared to a 24% increase in sales.

Gearing has decreased which means that the banks are not happy to lend money to the business.

- Gearing decreasing could be an indication that the company is less debt financed and more equity financed. It is believed that equity finance is less risky as you do not have to pay a dividend to the shareholders but you do have to pay interest on a loan.

My conclusion is that credit should be given.

(b) NOTE ONLY 3 external sources required. As this is worth 10 marks, students need to ensure they write at least 2–3 points on each source AND discuss ethical issues per the requirement.

Trade credit references/supplier references

Creditworthiness can be checked by asking the customer to supply trade references from other suppliers (usually two). It can be assumed that customers will not quote suppliers likely to give a bad report therefore it is unwise to rely on this procedure alone. Used in conjunction with other information, this procedure however may be helpful.

Bank references

Requests to the bank need to detail:

- the amount of credit you envisage giving the customer
- the credit period.

Bank replies are usually structured in one of three ways:

- an unqualified, positive assurance
- a general indication that the firm is operating normally
- a guarded statement, indicating that 'capital is fully employed' or 'we are unable to speak for your figures'.

Credit reference agency reports

The credit rating provided by the agency indicates the average amount of credit given to the firm. This helps the credit manager to assess the relative size of the proposed credit limit to the potential customer.

The problems with agency reports are as follows:

- New companies have no track record. It is therefore very difficult to form a judgement.
- It takes time for current information to be analysed and fed into computer/appraisal systems. It is possible for very relevant information (such as the collapse of a major customer) not to be in a report.

Management accounts

If available management accounts can be useful for identifying future plans (such as production and sales levels) of a company.

Credit circle meetings

A credit circle is a group of people with a common interest, for example a trade association. These people meet on a regular basis to share information on credit related matters, such as late payers.

Official publications

The press provide an up-to-date commentary on the situation within local and national companies. If the proposed customer is a big national company, reading The Financial Times enables the credit manager to keep up-to-date with half-yearly reports, comments on the customer as well as keeping abreast of industry trends and problems. Smaller more local companies are commented upon in regional and local papers.

Trade journals are often produced weekly or monthly. Trade journals are another valuable source of information and commentary on trends and results.

Ethical considerations

A credit controller must demonstrate objectivity when deciding whether to offer credit to a company. There are a number of ways in which a credit controller's objectivity could be threatened. These include:

The self-interest threat – a credit controller may be able to gain financially (or otherwise) if a request for credit is accepted. This could arise, for example, from a direct or indirect interest in the company or from fear of losing the business or having his, her or their employment terminated or as a consequence of undue commercial pressure from within or outside the firm.

The self-review threat – there will be a threat to objectivity if a decision to offer or decline credit made by the credit controller needs to be challenged or re-evaluated by him or her in the future.

The advocacy threat – there is a threat to a credit controller's objectivity if he, she or they becomes a supporter for or against the position taken by the company. The degree to which this presents a threat to objectivity will depend on the individual circumstances.

The familiarity or trust threat – the credit controller may be influenced by his, her or their knowledge of the company, may have a relationship with a member of staff at the company which could lead to the credit controller becoming too trusting.

The intimidation threat – the possibility that the credit controller may become intimidated by pressures, actual or feared, applied by the company or employer or by another.

TASK 4

(a) [2/(100 –2)] × [365/(28 – 14)] × 100 = **53.21%**

[1+2/(100 – 2)] ^ [365/(28 – 14)]–1 × 100 = **69.34%**

(b) **£9,300**

£10,000 – (£10,000 × £0.07) = £9,300

(c)

	True	False
The debt must be less than six month old		✓
The debt must be written off	✓	
The VAT should have been paid to HMRC	✓	

(d)

	Tick
Liquidity management is important so that the company can ensure that cash is available to discharge commitments.	✓
Liquidity management is important so that the company can estimate how much cash is tied up in inventory and non-current assets.	
Liquidity management is important to ensure that a company does not make a loss.	
Liquidity management is important so that the shareholders can see how much return they will get on their investment.	

(e) **£80,925**

£90,000 × 70% × 97.5% = £61,425 from month 4 sales

£65,000 × 30% = £19,500 from month 3 sales

Total cash = 61,425 + 19,500 = £80,925

(f) **£7,650**

VAT exclusive amount = £10,800 × 100/120 = £9,000. 85% of this is covered, £9,000 × 0.85 = £7,650.

(g) **A – Without recourse factoring**

The maximum amount that can be borrowed is **£600,000**. 80% of the outstanding balance is £600,400 which is greater than the maximum allowed.

TASK 5

(a) **D**

Simple claims between £10,000 and £25,000 are usually dealt with in the County Court under the Fast Track.

(b)

	True	False
The contract contains a retention of title clause and the goods have been delivered	✓	
The goods can be identified and have not been converted	✓	
The goods have been attached to an immoveable machine and are part of the machine		✓
The goods subject to the clause must be in the customers possession		✓

(c) **A**

As the goods have been delivered, the supplier wishes to be paid and so will take action for price. Damages might be an additional remedy because of the problems in obtaining payment, but would not be the main action. The supplier would not wish to repudiate the contract unless the goods could be recovered and, even then, would probably want some recompense for the inconvenience. Specific performance is more relevant to the customer obtaining goods from the supplier.

(d) **A**

(e) **B**

(f) The regular review of the aged trade receivable analysis should highlight customers who **have recent debts cleared but have older outstanding amounts**

The credit manager needs to be looking for customers who are building up a significant outstanding account

Analysis of trade receivables can be simplified using **Pareto's Principle**

If this principle is applied to the trade receivables of a company it could help the credit manager focus the credit control team. The credit manager could assume that **80% of the debts owed in value were due to only 20% of the customer accounts**

(g)

	Tick
Bankruptcy order	
Petition to the Court	✓
Appointment of Administrator	
Statutory demand	✓

TASK 6

(a) NOTE – With 10 marks available and two customers to discuss, students need to be putting 5–6 marks per customer. Make sure you mention what should have already happened, as well as what actions to take. Where possible, calculate values for the amounts to be provided for, claimed from credit insurance and reclaimed from HMRC. If no insurance claim can be made, ensure you state this clearly along with the reasons why not.

Duckula

- Under the terms and conditions any fault should have been notified to Bowler Limited within 24 hours of receipt.
- The account should be placed on stop.
- If they wish to keep the goods then Bowler Ltd can enforce the contract for payment.
- A provision for the debt should be made.
- If Bowler Ltd believes that the debt will not be paid even if the error was down to Duckula then it may be more beneficial for Bowler Ltd to collect the goods and resell them rather than try and collect the debt.
- If the error was made by Bowler Ltd then the goods should be collected and a credit note should be raised.
- In addition if the error is due to Bowler Ltd then they should waive the administration charge.
- Bowler may decide that as a goodwill gesture the administration charge will be waived, and also perhaps the collection fee.
- It may be that the customer's profitability in the course of the year is many times the additional cost if Bowler waives the charges.

Clanger

- All products manufactured by Bowler Ltd have a batch number stamped on them and so they should be easily identifiable.
- Receivers often attempt to avoid ROT claims by initially stating that the claim is not valid in the hope that the supplier will not pursue the claim any further.
- The threat of legal action can be used if the receiver is not cooperating with a possible identification visit.
- The credit insurance company often have a specialist insolvency section who themselves are often ex insolvency practitioners/specialists.
- Bowler Ltd or the credit insurer should therefore visit Clangers premises immediately to identify any goods still on the premises so that an ROT claim can be made.
- The receiver should be present to confirm identification if possible.
- The credit insurer should be contacted and a claim made for £30,000, provision for an irrecoverable debt of £10,000 should be made and VAT of £8,000 will be reclaimable from HMRC.

(b) Greenback

	£		£
01/04	20,000	15/04 (2,500 × 95%)	2,375
05/04	7,500	20/04	10,000
		Balance as at 30/04	**15,125**

	£		£
1/05	15,125	**Balance as at 31/05**	**27,625**
12/05	12,500		